Kidding Around

connecting kids to happiness, laughter and humour

An activity-based book for teachers and adults to use with kids of all ages— and even for their own well being.

Nat! to a fellow comedy believer! Sue

Sue Stephenson

illustrated by Tony MacKinnon

Printed and Distributed in Canada
Volumes
907 Frederick Street, Unit 8
Kitchener ON N2B 2B9
Canada
1-888-571-2665 OR 1-519-571-1908
www.volumesdirect.com

FIN 19 09 2018

Library and Archives Canada Cataloguing in Publication

Stephenson, Susan, 1948-, author
Kidding around : connecting kids to happiness, laughter and humour / Susan Stephenson.

ISBN 978-1-896080-11-6 (pbk.)

Also available as an ebook from www.amazon.com

1. Humor in children. 2. Child mental health.
3. Well-being. 4. Laughter--Psychological aspects.
5. Happiness--Psychological aspects. I. Title.

BF723.H85S74 2013 155.4'18 C2012-908404-2

Dedication

This book is dedicated to my two grandchildren—Katie and Matt—with all my love. They have both taught me so much about life!

1 800 668 6868
KidsHelpPhone.ca
Kids Help Phone

A portion of the sale of each copy will be donated to ***Kids Help Phone.***

Each section brings together information, inspiring quotes and stories to help you understand the importance of laughter and humour to kids' emotional and physical well-being. We all have concerns about our young people's mental health and the anxiety and stress they experience, and this book addresses these areas as well, including a section on bullying prevention and intervention. —Sue Dunlop, Principal

The book contains humour and research-based evidence that explain why happiness, laughter and humour are important AND contains activities that will help you incorporate more happiness and laughter into your own life and into the lives of your family, friends and students. In addition, Stephenson includes lists of resources such as books, apps, dvds and games as well as websites, like the one that made me laugh so hard.

This book won't make it onto my book shelf; it will stay on my desk so that I can refer to it often. —Debbie Axiak, teacher

Sue Stephenson has again written a relevant and unique book that contains great information along with fun activities that can easily be incorporated into the classroom. Sometimes, we need to be reminded that humour is an invaluable resource that makes teaching and learning a rich experience.
—Marilyn Orszulik, teacher

Susan (aka Sue) Stephenson loved going to school so much (no kidding around) that she became a Family Studies teacher, then an educational consultant and then a principal—always optimistic about universal success for all kids. Her keynotes and workshops focus on her passion for happiness & laughter, teamwork & trust . Sue is warmly welcomed by a wide variety of audiences in corporate, community and educational settings where she cleverly combines laughing with learning—a foolproof recipe for a living room, classroom or a bored room. She's not joking when she says we all need to lighten up, laugh more and look on the bright side of life.

Sue is a Certified Laughter Leader with the World Laughter Tour—or "certifiable" as her husband Tom says. Sue lives in Cobourg, Ontario, Canada. She serves as Executive Director and Board Member of **Stand UP for Student Well Being**, a registered charity. www.suswb.ca (formerly known as **Happiness at School**)

To order copies of Sue's books, please visit the website.

Website **www.suestephenson.ca**
LinkedIn **Susan Stephenson**
Telephone **1 647 400 2801**
Email **suestephenson@rogers.com**

Books also by Susan Stephenson:

- **Leading with Trust: How to Build Strong School Teams** (2009). Available in print version
- **Laughing Matters! Strategies for Building a Joyful Learning Community** (co-authored with Paul Thibault). (2006). Available as an ePub version or print version
- **Bromeando: como conectar a los niños con la felicidad, la risa y el humor.** (Spanish language version of Kidding Around) is available as an ePub version or print version

Table of Contents

Activity Summary List by Page

Part One: Put On A Happy Face

Part Two: LOL—Laughing Out Loud

Part Three: Loosen Up Your Funny Bones

Acknowledgements

The process of writing and formatting this book has been a combination of two different experiences. I often felt very isolated and alone (which is a challenge for an extravert), but I was strengthened by the supportive team that I had beside me whenever I needed their skills. Each member of this team played a vital role with his or her kindness and expertise.

Thanks to my team!

- Tom Milner—my husband, not only for his computer savvy and answers to my many questions but also most of all for his patience with this project.

- Susan Chisholm—for encouraging me with steady, sensible support through the entire process, clarifying the structure of the book and editing my writing.

- Tony MacKinnon (aka MAC)—for his skill in drawing the numerous artworks that communicate my messages so clearly —and for being the best brother-in-law.

- Doug Cornell—for his professional insight and feedback that kept me focused on the reality of the lives of today's parents and teachers and for shaping the manuscript with me for the ultimate audience of kids.

- Val and Gord McGiverin—for their invaluable ideas about the structure of the book and enthusiastic contributions to the overall project.

- Chris Higgins—for her excitement when talking about her granddaughter Miley that kept me going each time she gently offered her thoughts and reflected on my progress.

- Wendy O'Neill—for her confidence in me and her expert advice along the way.
- Ed Levy—for his editing skills and comments at a critical time in the process.
- Ardeth Staz—for her expertise and realistic feedback on this special project as we worked together.
- Pascale Guillotte—for her gentle facilitation between the team at *Kids Help Phone* and me.
- Anthony at the Apple Store for his help in finding solutions while working with the program Pages on my MacBook.
- Jane Cutler—for her "eagle-eye" in the final proofreading.
- Cheryl Lenser—for her skill as an indexer.
- David Chilton—author of *The Wealthy Barber Returns*, for his timely advice about the self-publishing industry.
- Jeff Kramer—for his assistance with the Roy Rogers Trust/ Estate.
- Jenn Sallans—for her trustworthy support at *Volumes*, the printer of the book

And to these four additional reviewers who guided my thinking in their own special ways: Tom Hierck, Elizabeth McFarlane, Marilyn Orszulik, and Donna Reist.

The Set-Up

Unity

I dreamed I stood in a studio and watched two sculptors there.

The clay they used was a young child's mind and they fashioned it with care.

One was a teacher, the tools he used were books, music and art.

The other, a parent, worked with a guiding hand and a gentle loving heart.

Day after day, the teacher worked with a touch that was deft and sure,

While the parent standing by his side polished and smoothed it o'er.

And when at last their task was done, they were proud of what they had wrought,

For the things they had molded into the child could neither be sold nor bought.

And they each agreed they would have failed if each had worked alone,
For behind the teacher stood the school, and behind the parent, the home.

—Source Unknown

About This Book

We need to get happiness, laughter and humour back into kids' lives. In our 21st century world, media, particularly social media, guarantee that today's children are bombarded with serious and even frightening issues that they need help navigating. Bullying, gangs and even terrorism were unimaginable for most of today's adults when they were young. Yet, those of us who deal with kids on a regular basis tend to focus on these matters to the exclusion of things that make life lighter and provide balance.

This book helps you teach children and teens about the benefits of happiness, humour and laughter in their lives, as well as how to deal with those days when they're angry, sad, or just stressed out. Learning more about having a positive outlook, and everything that goes along with it, is a lifelong skill with significant physical, psychological and sociological benefits—including doing better at school and in life.

Happiness is just one of many emotions, all of which are valid and have important lessons to teach us. This book will focus on happiness, but this does not mean that other emotions are not equally important. There are no good or bad feelings—all feelings have a place.

The book's three main parts contain information, practical activities and resources for adults to use with children—and even themselves.

Part One: Put on a Happy Face

Part One traces the Happiness Movement and positive psychology around the world. After introducing the Happiness Line (used throughout the book), this part explores sources of intrinsic and extrinsic happiness, explains feelings of sadness and unhappiness and provides strategies to help kids cope with unpleasant feelings.

Part Two: LOL—Laughing Out Loud

Part Two uses the Laughter Ladder to explain the range of laughter. It identifies twenty-one benefits of laughter and organizations that help continue the laughter, along with activities to get kids laughing.

Part Three: Loosen Up Your Funny Bones

Part Three introduces kids to the funny bone and its role in a playful attitude in life. This part outlines stages of humour development, explains differences between humour and comedy and includes a detailed description of both writers and performers of comedy.

It also addresses bullying as an issue to face when teasing becomes more serious and shares strategies for kids who observe bullying or experience bullying, in addition to ideas for families and kids to find help and turn around kids who bully.

The conclusion of each part contains implementation suggestions at three levels: (1) testing the water, (2) getting your feet wet and (3) jumping in the deep end.

> *"All over the world, when asked what they want most from life—and what they want most for their children—people answered that they want happiness."* —Gretchen Rubin

I hope that the book will be a learning experience for adult readers as they try the activities before sharing them with children. Imagine the possibilities as you merge your own philosophy and experiences with the content and activities introduced here. We are never too old to be happy, have fun and reconnect with the child in all of us!

PSST! *In Canada we put another "u" in humour when we spell it. The extra "u" is a reminder to include yourself.*

1 800 668 6868
KidsHelpPhone.ca

Kids Help Phone

I have always been a big supporter of *Kids Help Phone* in its mission to improve the well-being of children and youth in Canada by providing them with anonymous and confidential professional counselling, referrals and information. Part of the sale of each copy of *Kidding Around* will be donated to *Kids Help Phone*.

- 24 percent of calls and online contacts relate to mental health, including stress and anxiety.
- 21 percent of calls relate to peer pressure and similar issues that involve other kids.
- 10 percent of calls relate to bullying.
- 3 percent of calls relate to school issues, changing school, academic problems, ADHD and other learning disabilities.

The Happiness Line

A graphic organizer that gives us an overview of a range of emotions is the Happiness Line below. This book is aimed mainly at the upper half of the Happiness Line—the happy part, although there are suggestions included for those times when we don't feel happy. This focus is based on the belief that we can benefit from a more positive outlook, find more balance, experience a feeling of control and learn to be happier, no matter how old we are.

10 Extremely happy (feeling ecstatic, joyous, fantastic)

9 Very happy (feeling really good, elated)

8 Pretty happy (spirits high, feeling good)

7 Mildly happy (feeling fairly good and somewhat cheerful)

6 Slightly happy (just a bit above normal)

5 Neutral (not particularly happy or unhappy)

4 Slightly unhappy (just a bit below neutral)

3 Mildly unhappy (just a bit low)

2 Pretty unhappy (somewhat "blue", spirits down)

1 Very unhappy (depressed, spirits very low)

0 Extremely unhappy (utterly depressed, completely down)

The Fordyce Emotions Survey. Michael Fordyce. *Social Indicators Research* 20,355-381. Jan. 28, 2006. Reprinted with permission from Springer Publishers.

For Moms, Dads, Grandparents and Care Providers

"Every child is born with abundant creative potential for laughter, fun, play, happiness and love. Any restraint on any of these has an adverse effect on the child's growth and development. Therefore, instead of growing out of the child, we should grow with the child." —Robert Holden

Have you ever noticed that your teenage daughter doesn't smile very much or that your grandson seems to worry about things that other kids his age ignore? Or perhaps you are caring for a child who has to spend a lot of time alone. This book is meant to be a flexible resource that will fill a gap in mainstream parenting advice. The ideas and activities are not rigidly sequenced. Dip into it in whatever order or intensity you want.

The activities in the book focus on three areas of child development:

a) Social/emotional development and mental health issues
b) Speech and language development
c) Cognitive development

Parents don't discuss mental health issues with their children—though 65 percent incorrectly assume their child will come to them with a problem.
—2012 RBC Children's Health Parents' Poll of 2568 Canadian parents in the summer of 2012

A companion poll done by Kids Help Phone shows 50 percent of children are most likely to confide in friends, 30 percent in their mother, 22 percent in a health professional and 10 percent in the father.

Parents have the toughest job in the world, and it's one that comes with no instruction manual or formal training. They learn to parent on the job, facing high expectations and a long list of responsibilities—more than they ever bargained for—but have no chance of promotion. Parents are a child's first and longest-lasting teacher.

Every child is different, even within the same family, each having unique strengths and needs. As parents guide children through all the stages of development, moms and dads learn so many lessons, sometimes the hard way. While they are surrounded by messages in the media to be perfect super moms and super dads, parents are only human. They will make mistakes along the way. A sense of humour and the ability to laugh at their mistakes and learn from them will play a large role in their success as parents.

The ultimate goal for all parents is to nurture their children's individuality, independence and pride and help them be more resilient to become the best people they can be and to bounce back from those inevitable terrible days. When kids learn about trust, hope, optimism and confidence they are more able to cope with stress and resist depression.

Many grandparents also jump in to help out with grandchildren, giving parents support and encouragement. In some extended families, the grandparents live with the family in one house.

Parents can make the book's activities daily discussion topics around the dinner table, on car trips, during family meeting time, on rainy days or at bedtime. When kids are sick, an activity in the book might brighten their spirits and help them think of other things. Moms and dads can send the activity guide with them to camp, a friend's house or when they visit relatives.

Using this book and the activities with kids or grandkids will provide many unforgettable moments. All of the activities may not be funny, but they will open up a way to talk with kids about life more closely and candidly. Kids need to know they can talk with their parents about anything—that nothing is taboo or nondiscussable. Parents know their children the best and can assess when the time is right to introduce an activity or to save it for later. Even just having these topics close to one's own "funny bone" will help parents communicate about laughter and humour. Kids may say surprising things about many of these topics. Small changes in the activities and discussions can have big payoffs. Being there and being aware of their kids' behaviour will produce strong, long-lasting bonds.

Parents may even want to start a laughter journal, blog or video log to record things as mementos. Above all, parents should aim to be a role model for the behaviour they want to see in the children around them.

After parents, teachers have the second toughest job in the world. Both need more in-depth training to identify children's emotional issues as early as possible. Parents and teachers need to develop strong partnerships and support each other.

For Teachers and Other Educators

Schools ought to be naturally happy places by design. A sense of humour has been consistently rated by students as a top characteristic of good classroom teachers. After four decades of being a classroom teacher, a staff developer and a principal working with educators, I am convinced that including lighthearted fun and laughter in planning, instruction and assessment creates the potential to greatly reduce the anxiety felt by students. Students learn more and enjoy teachers who do three things: teach a rigorous curriculum, demand high standards and **have fun doing it**. — Stephenson and Thibault, 2006.

In a classroom energized by laughter, students:
- Are more motivated and attentive
- Feel a connection to the teacher
- Are more willing to take risks
- Have a safe and fun place to learn
- Are relaxed, comfortable and less stressed
- Are more creative and divergent thinkers, and
- Learn faster and retain it longer!

How You Teach Is As Important As What You Teach

"Sometimes to get the "ah-ha", you need to have the "ha-ha!" —Judy Siegel, writer

Humour is a powerful component of a wider range of instructional strategies. Some teachers use it naturally. Discover what's comfortable for you. When students learn with laughter, they not only feel better and have healthy coping skills for the stress in their lives, their achievement increases.

Helen Johnson, a British educator and administrator, makes a radical case for measuring the degree of laughter and emotional resilience of children in the culture of a school or classroom, in addition to the current focus on what she calls "performativity"—the assessment of performance through test scores of numeracy and literacy.

Teachers and other educators will find that the suggestions in the book easily integrate with various curriculum areas in reading, writing, oral language, media literacy, class community-building, character education, special education, social science, guidance, science, health, wellness and bullying prevention. It will complement initiatives such as safe schools, equity and social justice. Educators can consider using it as a unit or theme for a whole year.

"Laughing contributes to good mind and body balance," says Michael Lovorn, a humour researcher and teacher from CSU Long Beach. "It makes students ready to learn and helps teachers rise above the assembly-line mentality. In an age of so-called failing schools, we should keep in mind that human beings have laughed longer than they've been tested, and that everybody appreciates being in an environment that is welcoming and conducive to putting smiles on their faces".—"Laughter Makes You Smarter", California Teachers' Association. Vol. 13, Issue 4, Dec. 2008/Jan. 2009

Messages Adults Send to Kids

Maya Angelou, an American author and poet, tells us that our face should light up whenever we see a child. We are often too serious as adults. In the busyness of a hectic day, we can lose our patience and snap at children seeking our attention. We need to use the word "no" only in dangerous situations and to set limits. More often than not, we can choose to communicate messages in a positive way.

You may even remember hearing these frightening comments when you were young. Do they sound familiar?

Grow up and act your age! You think this is funny, do you? Learn to control yourself. Quit clowning around. Wipe that stupid smile off your face. Stop laughing and grow up. Save your good toys for later. Clean up your room and then you can play. You'll be sorry. Get a grip. Cut it out. Just wait 'til your father gets home. How dare you speak to me like that. You're driving me nuts.

On the other hand, there are many ways to praise and encourage the behaviour of a child—and get a smile in return. Children need to know that they do indeed deserve good things.

Awesome. You mean the world to me. You're fantastic. Dynamite. Hip, hip hooray. How smart. I knew you could do it. Neat. Looking good. Now you've got it. You're incredible. Outstanding. That's correct. You're a joy. That's the best. Nothing can stop you now. You are fun to be with. You're A-OK. You mean a lot to me. You're on your way. You brighten my day. Wonderful. Keep going. Excellent. Now you're talking. Every time I see you, I'm thankful. I appreciate your contribution.

The Word in Your Heart

Canadian author Robertson Davies asked some graduating students in a commencement speech, "As you come up to accept your diploma, what is the word in your heart? Is it no, or is it yes?" Martin Seligman, a former President of the American Psychological Association, says in *Authentic Happiness,* that this question sums up twenty years of his work.

Seligman puts it this way: "I believe there is a word in your heart, and that this is not a sentimental fiction. I don't really know where this word comes from, but one of my guesses is that it forms drop by drop from the words we hear from our parents. If a child hears an angry 'no' at every turn, when she approaches a new situation she will be anticipating a 'no', with all the associated freezing and lack of mastery."
—Seligman, 2002, p. 218.

Encourage your child to hear "yes" in his or her heart. Take some time to have some fun with the children in your life. It's so easy to deflate the mood of a happy day and change a child's smile to a frown with just one admonishing sentence.

It is just as important to be there for kids in their sad days. Adults, especially parents, need to listen to kids talk about their feelings and to reach out and ask questions if they suspect there are problems. Many kids are skilled at hiding what's really going on inside and yet desperately want someone to talk with. Never underestimate the power of what you do and say with children.

Cautionary Note: It is beyond the scope and intent of this book to address extreme unhappiness, or to guide you in how to care for or treat a deeply depressed child or teen. If a few days of sadness extend into weeks of depression, there are other people and resources who can help.

In such cases, church leaders, community agencies and support workers, guidance counsellors, assistant principals and principals and, of course, teachers the child connects with are great people to start with. They may refer you to psychologists and other medical doctors.

Use your judgment as to when the activities in this book might help a child who is feeling very sad. Above all, do no harm. Be sensitive to children's feelings, and be ready for spontaneous, unexpected reactions along with the opportunity to have some fun.

Thunderstorms, Fudge and Honky-Tonk Music

Like everything we do in life, the roots of this book stem from personal experience. The following story is a vivid memory that stays with me to this day and illustrates the profound impact the words and actions of parents and the power of shared fun and laughter.

I am the oldest of three girls (and the oldest grandchild) in our family and have always taken that responsibility seriously. When I was about eight years old, I was frightened of loud thunderstorms and lightning, especially at night. My mother first tried a scientific explanation to dispel my fear. Then she tried watching the storm with me and counting how many seconds there were between the lightning and the thunder. Neither strategy worked. However, two things she thought of doing really did work!

We had a record player and a favourite album (yesterday's equivalent of the mp3 payer and music files) that consisted of honky-tonk music—lively, rhythmic piano songs. When it started thundering and lightning outside, she would put on that album and crank up the volume, and my sisters and I would dance wildly around our little house, up to the second floor and down to the basement many times.

I also remember my mother taking out a saucepan and ingredients to whip up a batch of fudge during storms. We would take turns stirring the mixture over the sink. Imagine that! Dance music and fudge—together they were so much fun! Looking back, I realize how ingenious it was of my mother to do something that was fun (and yummy too) to take my mind off the storm and ease my anxiety. Even to this day, when there is a thunderstorm, I think of being a kid again and turn on some dancing music—but my husband Tom doesn't make fudge.

Over the years, laughter has become a focus of my life. I loved my career with parents, kids and teachers. Like many others, I need to lighten up and remind myself to be happy every day.

Part One

Put On A Happy Face

"Gray skies are gonna clear up, Put on a happy face
Brush off the clouds and cheer up, Put on a happy face."

—from the song "Put On a Happy Face" by Lee Adams and Charles Strouse, from the musical *Bye, Bye Birdie.*

Happiness is a word we use so often that it can seem superficial, but it does have a deeper and more complex meaning. Do we need to be laughing and having fun to be happy? Do we need to have relationships with other people to be happy? Does being rich and famous bring happiness? This chapter introduces the discipline of happiness and how to develop it as a lifelong skill.

The Happiness Movement

"Since the eighteenth century the pursuit of happiness has gained momentum and spread to every aspect of behavior, from religion and politics to work and parenting." —Peter Stearns

In the United States Americans embedded the pursuit of happiness, along with life and liberty, in their Declaration of Independence as a fundamental right. But happiness sometimes proceeds along less lofty and more pragmatic lines. Advances in human comfort such as better home heating made life more comfortable. Improved dentistry made it more likely to see people smile and reveal their teeth.

Historically, there wasn't much of a connection between happiness and child development until the early twentieth century. From the 1920s on, child-rearing manuals started to emphasize the importance of being happy and how to achieve it.

In 1963, advertising executive Harvey Ball created the yellow smiley face which has an annual licensing revenue of over $50 million. After he died in 2001, the Harvey Ball Foundation was created to honour his name and memory. World Smile Day is the first Friday in October each year. Visit www.worldsmileday.com

Since the year 2000, we have witnessed what could be called a happiness movement marked by an explosion of articles and books on this topic. The serious study of happiness is leading to more and more scientific research and a separate discipline to be studied. It's about time! The most popular class at Harvard University today is the Happiness Class, with over one thousand students.

Happiness Around the World

In a January-February 2012 article in the *Harvard Business Review*, titled "The History of Happiness", Peter N. Stearns tells us that cultural variations in happiness are considerable. For example, he writes that "when MacDonald's arrived in Russia in 1990, one of its first tasks was to train clerks to seem cheerful." Russians were less carefree and smiled less than Western cultures. East Asian cultures have lower happiness expectations than Americans. On the other hand, Latin American cultures have higher happiness expectations. Not only do levels of happiness vary around the world, but they can also change over the years.

The report of the Organisation for Economic Co-operation and Development (OECD) on life satisfaction in the developed world finds that economic prosperity, health and a strong social network continue to correspond highly with happiness. The OECD measures more than thirty sets of data in eleven different categories. In the 2012 report, Denmark continued to rank as the happiest country in the world, in part because multiple families often live together in co-housing units along with their elders and because Danes report having the most leisure time available per day. 24/7 Wall St. reviewed the ten countries in which residents reported personal well-being at an average of 7.2 out of 10 or better. The countries of Norway, Netherlands, Switzerland, Austria, Israel, Finland, Australia, Canada and Sweden ranked second to tenth after Denmark. The USA ranked eleventh in life satisfaction. (*The Happiest Countries in the World.* 24/7 Wall St., May 22, 2012.) Researchers have begun to differentiate surveys that measure life satisfaction or happiness from those emphasizing material satisfactions. More sophistication in the data will emerge as measures to rate happiness are perfected over time.

Just as happiness levels can differ between countries and cultures, happiness levels can differ among children in the same family, among families and schools in the same community and among regions of the same country.

Positive Psychology

"For every one hundred articles on sadness, there is just one on happiness."—Martin Seligman

The Happiness Movement brought with it a new field focused on an interest in well-being and living better lives. Martin Seligman coined the phrase "positive psychology" and provided a refreshing way to look at our feelings, especially happiness. He said in 2005, "I realized that my profession was half-baked. It wasn't enough for us to nullify disabling conditions. . . .We needed to ask, what are the enabling conditions that make human beings flourish?"—"The New Science of Happiness," *Time*, C. Wallis, Jan. 9, 2005.

Let's think about happiness and sadness in a slightly different way by using the Happiness Line as shown in the following scale:

The Happiness Line

10 Extremely happy (feeling ecstatic, joyous, fantastic)

9 Very happy (feeling really good, elated)

8 Pretty happy (spirits high, feeling good)

7 Mildly happy (feeling fairly good and somewhat cheerful)

6 Slightly happy (just a bit above normal)

5 Neutral (not particularly happy or unhappy)

4 Slightly unhappy (just a bit below neutral)

3 Mildly unhappy (just a bit low)

2 Pretty unhappy (somewhat "blue", spirits down)

1 Very unhappy (depressed, spirits very low)

0 Extremely unhappy (utterly depressed, completely down)

The Fordyce Emotions Survey. Michael Fordyce. *Social Indicators Research* 20,355-381. Jan. 28, 2006. Reprinted with permission from Springer Publishers.

The bottom of the line (zero) represents people with feelings of sadness, depression or being "down". This can happen for many reasons. Some people (called "happy-chondriacs") feel they are not meant to be happy, and live in fear of happiness.

If we feel just OK or neutral (not particularly happy or unhappy), we are in the middle of the line (at 5). When we are feeling extremely happy, ecstatic, joyous and fantastic, we are at the top end of the Happiness Line (at 10). Research done by Ed Diener, the author of 240 scientific publications on the topic, reports that most people are mildly happy most of the time.

It can help to assign numbers to places along the line, so we could say, for example, "I am at 7 today", to help ourselves and others figure out what kind of day it is in "our world". Teachers and parents could use a large wall chart of the Happiness Line on the bulletin board or on the fridge so children can start putting words to their "place on the line".

It's normal to move up and down on the Happiness Line daily or weekly, because our moods or emotional states change and things happen to us and our families that are sad or happy. You don't want children to pretend to be happy. That would be phony and artificial and would cause more stress. We all have to deal with anxiety, anger, frustration and sadness. The Happiness Line helps children start to think more deeply about this range of feelings.

It's important to know that, if you end up stuck at zero for more than a few weeks, you need to reach out and get some help.

"For every minute you are angry you lose sixty seconds of happiness."
— Ralph Waldo Emerson

Our Happiness Range

Our total amount of happiness can be divided into three parts:
a) our genetic set range—about 50 percent
b) our life circumstances—about 10 percent
c) our voluntary choices—about 40 percent

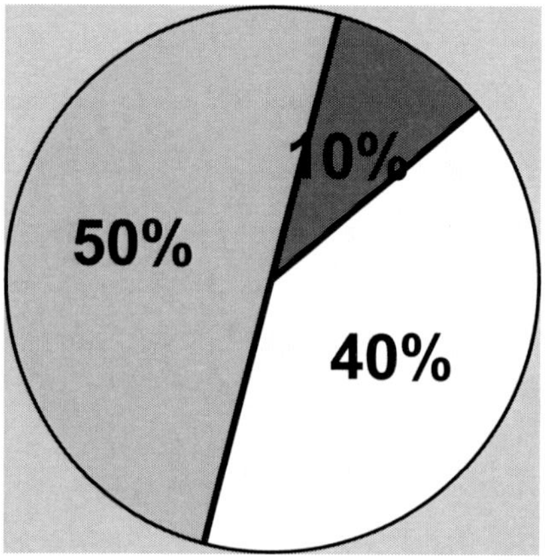

Each of us has a certain emotional range or area on the Happiness Line where we "hang out" most of the time. Seligman calls this our "set range" and says that 50 percent of our happiness potential is predetermined, inherited through our genes from our birth parents. In fact, studies conducted on the personality development of twins and adopted children show that "the psychology of identical twins turns out to be much more similar than that of fraternal twins, and the psychology of adopted children turns out to be much more similar to their biological parents than to their adoptive parents"—Seligman, 2002, p.47.

Life circumstances include the country we live in and the family we have. Circumstances can improve happiness for the better, although it may be difficult or expensive to do so. They make up about 10 percent of our happiness. Surprisingly, education, race, financial income, gender and climate don't affect happiness a great deal.

The really good news is that the third category of voluntary choices, the way we act and think, is largely within our control. The effort required may be great, but the result will be more lasting. What type of and how many friends do you want to have? What will you spend your money on? How will you deal with the sad times you encounter? What type of language do you use? Are you pessimistic or optimistic? Do you reach out and help others in your community? These voluntary choices are the basis of this book.

"We either make ourselves miserable or we make ourselves happy. The amount of work is the same." —Carlos Castaneda

Let's use a trampoline to represent the amount of happiness we inherit from our birth parents. It's a given weight and size we cannot change—like the weather, where we live and our own level of energy. We have so many choices—how often we use the trampoline, if we ask friends to join us, how high we can jump—and how safe we are while we use our trampoline.

"Happy people are more altruistic, more productive, more helpful, more likable, more creative, more resilient, more interested in others, friendlier, and healthier. Happy people make better friends, colleagues and citizens." —Gretchen Rubin

These positive effects are a dramatic argument for studying and understanding happiness.

Activity: My Happiness Line Survey

Study the range of feelings on the Happiness Line with children so they become familiar with the levels from 0-10.

- Take a quick happiness survey. Ask children to select their own current happiness point on the line. Talk about their decision. What range is normal for them—for example, between 4 and 8?
- Ask kids to start to think about how often they feel happy (6 or above), neutral (at 5) or unhappy (4 or below). Where do they hang out the most?
- Ask kids to think of a time when they were at 10, 5 and 0 on the Happiness Line. Can they describe a situation for each one in a drawing or in a few sentences? What was happening? Can they recall specific details?
- Ask a wider group of kids where they are on the line. There is always a range of feelings in any group and it will be interesting for kids to experience this.

Kids could get to know the feelings associated with different points on the line and start to refer to them by number. Teachers could place Happiness Lines on each desk so that students could nonverbally indicate where they are when they arrive in the morning and where they move during the day. Make a larger chart or poster for the house or classroom so the Happiness Line becomes a visual aid for everyone to use on a daily basis. This would help teachers and parents know when to press and when not to interrupt.

If You're Happy, Tell Your Face

Researchers have found that even by putting on a smile, you can feel happier. Have you ever made an effort to confront an unpleasant feeling just by smiling? Do you wake up each morning with a happy face or does it take a while to find it? Some people have naturally happier looking faces. Other people may appear to be frowning just by the natural shape of their mouth, even though they are actually happy. Our faces reveal to the world what kind of day we're having and how we're feeling. So, if you're happy, make sure you tell your face and share your smile!

Activity Reading Facial Expressions

What are the facial clues to feelings? Here are some questions for kids to think about:

- Do you think you can choose how you feel or which face you will put on?
- Are facial expressions and feelings contagious? Can they jump from one person to another?
- Try putting on a grumpy face or a mad face. How do you feel?
- Can you make yourself happier by changing a frown to a smile?
- Can you really put on a happy face if you don't feel it?
- In a group, play a game of charades where people make facial expressions that change their eyebrows, eyes and mouth. See how many faces other people can correctly identify (for example, excitement, pleasure, fear or disappointment).
- What do you think the rest of the body is doing with each of these four faces? Act out the body language that goes along with each one.

- Did making these facial expressions cause you to feel a bit of the feeling you were communicating?
- Have you ever found that you have misinterpreted a person's mood by his or her facial expression?

Activity Feelings and Faces Photo Search

Divide a piece of paper or a poster into four parts and label the four parts as mad, sad, OK and happy.

Use magazines, greetings cards and newspapers to find pictures for each feeling—or even draw them yourself.

Fill each part with pictures that fall into each category and glue them on the paper to make a collage.

Then sit back and ask yourself:
a) Was it more difficult to find any one of the four feelings and faces in your search?
b) How many happy faces did you find in the newspaper?

Note: Download and print the four faces at **www.suestephenson.ca** and use them as visual aids.

Emoticons

Emotions plus icons = emoticons. When we want to insert a quick pictorial symbol or icon into an email, web forum or text message to improve the communication of an emotion or make an exclamation, text emoticons are very useful. Vertical emoticons date back to 1881 with the use of __/! for a smiling mouth.
Western emoticons are usually read from left to right and require the reader to tilt his or her head 90 degrees to the left to read them. Scott Fahlman invented these two emoticons in

1982 to express emotion using punctuation marks to represent the eyes, nose and mouth.

:-) meant funny
;-(meant it is not a joke

There are hundreds of emoticons that can be used. Here are a few other examples. (These emoticons leave out the nose.)

: (means sad
;) means a wink
>:(means anger

When Harvey Ball created the small yellow smiley face with two black dots for eyes and a black smiling mouth in 1963, a new series of emoticons were inspired.

Activity **The Language of Emoticons**

a) Ask kids to study the above chart to see the many variations on one smiley face. There are thousands of other examples of emoticons on the Internet or cell phones.

b) Use a new version of the Happiness Line and place emoticons along the line. For example, what emoticon would best represent 7 on the line?

c) Ask kids to create their own emoticons for a range of emotions.

d) Discuss:

How they are currently used in communication
Why they are used instead of putting feelings in words
If they are used in hurtful ways in messages

Happy Talk

There's power in the language and words we choose to use when we're faced with a stressful or upsetting situation. Consider these two extremes.

At one end of the spectrum are people who tend to "see the glass half empty": the pessimists. Their frame of mind is rooted in a sense of hopelessness or, at best, a sense that the obstacles they face either can't be overcome or can only be overcome with great difficulty. Their vocabulary tends to focus on what's wrong with the world or why things can't be changed for the better. This pattern of grumbling, unhappy talk is called "kvetching" in Yiddish. It's true a good kvetch every now and then can relieve stress and identify a problem that needs to be addressed. However, if it becomes the permanent tone of a person's conversation, that negativity can be a powerful force.

At the other extreme, there are people who have a tendency to see the "glass half full". They expect the best outcome and more often get it. They are happier, more trusting and optimistic. They use a different sort of language that focuses more on problem-solving. Their first reaction to a troublesome situation may be to complain, but they soon get over that and try to do something in a productive way that's beneficial to themselves and to others.

Which type of language do you tend to use—happy talk or unhappy talk?

"Definition of an optimist: someone who figures that taking a step backward after taking a step forward is not a disaster, it's a cha-cha."
—Robert Brault, writer

Activity Listen to Your Language

In 2007 Rev. Will Bowen in Kansas City, Missouri started a "complaint-free challenge" for twenty-one days, asking his congregation to wear a little purple wrist bracelet and switch it to the other wrist whenever they caught themselves complaining. People who made it through the twenty-one days without complaining saw their stress levels drastically reduced and their relationships and happiness levels improved. Rev. Bowen even gave them Certificates of Happiness.

Try this yourself with a bracelet or piece of string. See how long you can last before you have to move the bracelet and how hard it is for you. In what situations is it harder to stay optimistic?

1. Brainstorm positive words you use to describe feelings of happiness. (Here are some examples: *delightful, blissful, gleeful, jovial, cheerful, joyful.*) Make an effort to use words like these more often each day.

2. Post them on cards or signs around the house or in the classroom for daily reminders.

3. Think about what words young children use for happiness. How about parents and grandparents? What words unique to your culture or family mean happiness? Listen to your family members for their Happy Talk.

Celebrations of Learning

As an example of the power of language, let's look at the negative associations kids often have with tests and exams at school. Even young students experience the anticipatory anxiety, stress and tension of knowing they are being assessed. We vividly remember this ourselves as students.

At a teachers' workshop I was co-leading a few years ago, a teacher told everyone how she reframed the negative anticipation students have with quizzes, tests and exams by calling them "Celebrations of Learning" instead! She gave her students party hats and noisemakers before the first test and introduced the celebration. From then on, everyone asked, "When are we having the next Celebration of Learning?"

Using humour and fun in assessment reduces anxiety and stress and improves:

- The connection between student and teacher
- Student responsiveness (keeps them awake!)
- Classroom atmosphere
- Self-esteem and motivation
- Mental functioning and performance
- Feelings of calmness and control
- Good feelings (releases endorphins)

Whether it's for a beginning, ongoing or final assessment, teachers can:

- Welcome students in a fun, encouraging way.
- Include funny directions, content and/or choices.
- Have a stretch break or create some excuse to move.
- Encourage a sense of humour in anecdotal comments.
- Return results with sensitivity, compassion and with respect to students' privacy.

More Isn't Always Better

Are the best things in life free? Can money really buy happiness? Do we have to postpone happiness to some time in the future when we have the bigger house or car, or a million in the bank? Or, might happiness be right here, right now, all around us?

Many Western children grow up dreaming of a successful future with all the big, expensive things. For decades Westerners have believed that social mobility and material wealth would bring happiness. But research tells us that beyond the provision of our basic needs, money has little or no effect on lasting happiness. Even people who win a large lottery return to their set range of happiness over time.—Seligman, 2002, p. 48. The excitement wears off once they have what they need.

Movie director Tom Shadyac learned this lesson firsthand. He is well known for such comedy films as *Liar Liar, The Nutty Professor, Bruce Almighty* and *Patch Adams.* He had been living in a 17,000-square-foot mansion, and had the glitzy Hollywood lifestyle that went along with it. It was the life many kids dream about. However, he had an uneasy, empty feeling that something wasn't right—he wasn't any happier with all these material belongings.

In 2007, Shadyac sold his mansion, moved into a modest mobile home and began giving away his fortune. In his own words: "I simply met myself at my needs." He confronted what his culture had taught him growing up and changed his values and behaviour. Not long after this decision, he was in a traumatic bike accident. During his recovery from post-concussion syndrome, he went through a phase that led him to face his own death and focus on his life purpose. At that time he made a documentary *I Am* to share his own struggle with what he could do to make the world a better place. He says in the documentary: "I was standing in the house that my culture had taught me was a measure of the good life. I was struck with one very clear, very strange feeling: I was no happier."—Shadyac, 2011 . Today he says he's never felt happier.

Back in 2005, when Shadyac was thinking about what was wrong with the world, he read an article claiming that the United States was twenty-third on a list of happiest countries. He took the article to his friend Roko Belic who subsequently spent six years exploring happiness around the world as director of the award-winning film *Happy*. Shadyac became the eventual executive producer of the movie.

One of the most revealing scenes was filmed in the slums of Kolkata, India. There, Belic found a man who had very few belongings, lived in a one-room home protected only by a plastic tarp and earned his wages pulling a rickshaw, and yet said he was happy and his life was good because he and his family had the essentials of life. Another segment of *Happy* takes us to Bhutan, a country nestled between India and China, where the government looks at Gross National Happiness (GNH) instead of Gross National Product (GNP). They place more value on what they can share than on what they have.

Belic found that people who value relationships and making the world a better place are happier than those whose goals focus more on money and fame.

While the radical shift taken by Shadyac made him happier, it may take a great deal of convincing to get most people to do the same. Watching a DVD called *Happy* will help make his case.

Note: The two movies *I AM* and *Happy* are available as DVDs to purchase. An educational edition of *Happy* is also available.

The Small Stuff Matters More

Just as happiness and unhappiness are at opposite ends of the Happiness Line, excitement and boredom are also opposites.

Excitement comes in many shapes for children and adults alike, from winning a big soccer game to the last day of school in June! You just have to watch fans in mind-blowing moments meeting their idols like Justin Bieber to see them shake and scream in an adrenaline rush. But after they're over, very few extremely exciting experiences have long-term effects. Excitement is often followed by a mood crash as reality takes over.

So it's not the intensity of a big, exciting experience but the frequency and number of the little things we often don't notice that matter. Happiness can be a calm, peaceful feeling and often involves appreciating the small things in life. Happiness is different than excitement.

"*Somebody who has a dozen mildly nice things happen each day is likely to be happier than somebody who has a single truly amazing thing happen.*" —Ed Diener, psychologist.

No one knows this better than Toronto's Neil Pasricha, the author of the international bestseller *The Book of Awesome* that grew out of a daily blog he wrote at the website www.1000awesomethings.com. Awesome in Pasricha's usage means full of awe, eliciting great respect and admiration. He says, "These tiny, little moments make an awesome difference for a boring guy with a nine-to-five job." —Pasricha, 2010.

Writing this blog was extremely therapeutic during a very rough patch in Pasricha's life and gave him a way out of the blues and into happiness.

Activity — My Awesome List

Here are some examples from *The Book of Awesome* to get kids started on their own awesome list. Ask kids to choose from the following list which ones might be in their own Book of Awesome.

- The smell of crayons
- Wearing warm underwear just out of the dryer
- Popping bubble wrap
- Someone landing on the hotel you just bought in Monopoly
- The sound of scissors cutting through construction paper
- When the socks from the dryer match up perfectly
- Being the first person in a really crowded movie theatre and getting prime seats
- The feeling of scrunching sand under your feet
- Picking up a *q* and a *u* at the same time in Scrabble
- Blowing out all the birthday candles on your first try
- A long hug when you really need it
- Building a stack of pancakes that looks just like the front of the box
- Absolute perfect silence
- When it feels like the lyrics of the song you are listening to were written just for you
- Hanging out with your mom or dad

Which ones would they add?

Some responses could be: going to the park, eating a chocolate bar, getting a higher mark on a school assignment than expected, listening to a favourite song or learning to ride a bike.

The Twenty-Four Signature Strengths

> *"We believe that you can get more satisfaction out of life if you identify which of these character strengths you have in abundance and then use them as much as possible in school, in hobbies, and with friends and family."*
> —Martin Seligman

Martin Seligman has three criteria for what he calls "signature strengths":

a) They are valued in almost every culture around the world.
b) They are valued in their own right.
c) They are malleable (capable of being shaped).

Following are his six core virtues subdivided into twenty-four strengths. (For a more detailed explanation of these strengths refer to Seligman's book *Authentic Happiness*, his newest book *Flourish*, or his website www.authentichappiness.com.)

1. Wisdom and Knowledge
a) Curiosity
b) Love of Learning
c) Judgment
d) Ingenuity
e) Social Intelligence
f) Perspective

2. Courage
g) Valor
h) Perseverance
i) Integrity

3. Humanity and Love
j) Kindness
k) Loving

4. Justice
l) Citizenship
m) Fairness
n) Leadership

5. Temperance (restraint)
o) Self-Control
p) Prudence (good judgment)
q) Humility

6. Transcendence
r) Appreciation of beauty
s) Gratitude
t) Hope
u) Spirituality
v) Forgiveness
w)Humour and Play
x) Zest

Activity — My Strengths Survey

There are two recent, web-based questionnaires available on the website www.authentichappiness.com that measure signature strengths: the Values in Action (VIA) Survey of Character Strengths for Adults and the VIA Strength Survey for Children eight to seventeen. 2.5 million people have taken these surveys!

Participants are instructed to read each statement, decide how much it fits them personally and mark the correct choice online. There are no right or wrong answers. Upon completion of the 198 questions, a ranked summary of the top five signature strengths is provided and compared to the other strengths. Although it appears to be a time-consuming test, it takes only between ten and fifteen minutes to complete.

Here are three sample questions:

- I like to think of different ways to solve a problem
- I complain more often than I feel grateful about my life
- When my friends are upset, I listen to them and comfort them.

The questions themselves, as well as the results, will be of great interest to children, especially in helping them see where they rank in the strength of "humor and play". The top five strengths are summarized when the survey is completed.

Parents could take the test as well, letting their answers reflect what they know about their child. Their results and the ones their child produced would make an interesting comparison. If at all possible, the previous year's teacher could provide useful insights.

In addition to discussing their reactions to these signature strengths with a parent or teacher, children could also expand on each strength by:

- Creating a visual depiction of a time when they have used this strength
- Orally telling a story
- Writing a story or poem
- Acting out a scenario
- Interviewing another family member to get his or her interpretation of the results of the survey for this child

Happiness Comes From Within

With real effort and perseverance, it is possible to move up the Happiness Line to the upper reaches of our set range. You cannot force yourself to be happy, but you can make the effort to get started. There are many healthy ways to do this. You can do small things consistently differently every day and wait for results. The next two activities in this chapter will collect the key learnings from the previous activities in Part One and culminate in a Happiness List Activity that will be helpful both in good and bad times.

It takes real effort to choose to be happy. Here is a list of ways to be happy that come from satisfactions that can't be bought as opposed to material sources of happiness. Experiment with this list and see what works for you. What would you add to or remove from the list?

1. Spend time with friends, family, and community members.
2. Get involved, volunteer, give back.
3. Watch for awesome things each day.
4. Try something new, novel and different.
5. Develop a better sense of humour to have more fun.
6. Let go of the negative.
7. Take your work seriously, but yourself more lightly.
8. Show up fully present and do your best each day.
9. Perform a random act of kindness to make someone's day.
10. Build your body strength by exercising, dancing, singing, walking, swimming or skateboarding.

11. Learn how to meditate to be calmer when stressed.
12. Create something—knit, invent, build, dance, paint, cook.

In her best-selling book, *The Happiness Project,* Gretchen Rubin teaches us valuable lessons she learned from researching what could make her happier. Each month for a year she focused on a different area. Rubin's process can be used by children as young as kindergarten age. Everyone's project will be unique, and almost everyone will benefit from starting one.

The steps she took over her year-long exploration have been adapted here for kids embarking on their Own Happiness Project Activity.

Activity — My Happiness Project

1. Start by deciding on a list of a few areas you could work on to continue to be happy or maybe feel happier. For Rubin, these were simple activities—for example, making time for friends, boosting her energy and being serious about play.

To do this she suggests answering these four questions:

a) What makes you *feel good*? What activities do you find fun, satisfying, or energizing?
b) What makes you *feel bad*? What are the sources of anger, irritation, boredom, frustration and anxiety in your life?
c) Is there any way in which you don't *feel right* about your life?
d) Do you have ways to produce an *atmosphere of growth*? In what elements of your life do you find progress, learning, challenge, improvement and increased mastery?

2. Once you are settled on the one or two areas you need to work on that will make you happier, develop a Happiness Project Chart for each area as shown in an example on page 38. Let's use the example of "making new friends." Two

specific and measurable, happiness-boosting resolutions for this area could be:

- Talk with Marty (who is someone I like but don't know very well) at recess or lunch. Learn some new things about him and share some things about myself.
- Join the media club after school to find someone who is also interested in computer animation.

Each resolution has to be very specific and measurable. Keep track on the Happiness Project Chart your degree of success using one of these three symbols:

+	(excellent results)
✓	(good results)
—	(no evidence)

Do this each day for twenty-one days in a row. (Twenty-one consecutive days are needed to solidify a new habit.)

Rubin's reason for calling them resolutions instead of goals is important. She says, "You hit a goal. You keep a resolution." So make positive resolutions you will keep, instead of goals you want to attain.

Sample Page: **My Happiness Project**

Area: *Make more friends*

Resolution 1: *Talk with Marty (who is someone I like but don't know very well) at recess or lunch. Learn some new things about him and share some things about myself.*

1	2	3	4	5	6	7	8	9	10	11	12	13	14	15	16	17	18	19	20	21
+	+	✓	✓	-	-	✓	+	✓	✓	✓	+	✓	✓	✓	-	✓	✓	✓	+	++

Use a + (excellent results), ✓(good results), or a — (no evidence) each day for 3 weeks.

Resolution 2: *Join the media club after school to find someone who is also interested in computer animation.*

1	2	3	4	5	6	7	8	9	10	11	12	13	14	15	16	17	18	19	20	21
✓	✓	✓	✓	✓	✓	+	+	+	✓	✓	-	-	✓	+	+	+	+	+	+	+

Use a + (excellent results), ✓(good results), or a — (no evidence) each day for 3 weeks.

> *"The feeling of control is an essential element of happiness—a better predictor of happiness than, say, income. Having a feeling of autonomy, of being able to choose what happens in your life or how you spend your time, is crucial. Identifying and following my resolutions had made me far more in control of my time, my body, my actions, my surroundings, and even my thoughts. Getting control of my life was definitely an aspect of my happiness project, and a greater feeling of control gave me a major boost in happiness."*
> —Gretchen Rubin

Use the steps that Rubin followed and experiment with what makes YOU happy. What makes "your heart sing"? You will feel better when you are doing what you really love and are passionate about.

Remember that happiness doesn't necessarily equate with fun or laughter; some people find their work or what they are learning at school makes them happy—so much so, it feels like play at times.

It may take a few rough drafts to get this into the shape you want it to be. When you are happy with it, use page 40 for your final copy.

How well did you do? Should you repeat the Happiness Project with another area and resolutions or have you learned enough?

Note: Please see the Happiness Project Starter Kit on her website. She is trying to maintain a list of all the Happiness Project groups. Please take her six-question survey about your group at http://bit.ly/ijiJOy. To see a list of other Happiness Project groups, check out the Happiness Project Groups tab on her blog. Gretchen Rubin invites emails at grubin@gretchenrubin.com

"Most folks are about as happy as they make up their minds to be."
—Abraham Lincoln, former United States President

Activity Chart: **My Happiness Project**

Area____

Resolution 1______________________________________

1	2	3	4	5	6	7	8	9	10	11	12	13	14	15	16	17	18	19	20	21

Use a + (excellent results), ✓(good results), or a — (no evidence) each day for 3 weeks.

Resolution 2______________________________________

1	2	3	4	5	6	7	8	9	10	11	12	13	14	15	16	17	18	19	20	21

Use a + (excellent results), ✓(good results), or a — (no evidence) each day for 3 weeks.

Resolution 3______________________________________

1	2	3	4	5	6	7	8	9	10	11	12	13	14	15	16	17	18	19	20	21

Use a + (excellent results), ✓(good results), or a — (no evidence) each day for 3 weeks.

—Permission to print this chart granted from Gretchen Rubin

Whatever happiness is for you, find positive ways to be happy and have fun. Be happy with yourself—in your own skin. Be yourself. Give yourself permission to be happier.

As you conduct your three-week Happiness Project, you will discover what works and what doesn't work for you. Remember that everyone is different, so be honest with yourself.

Activity Happiness Is…

Watch a version of the song "Happiness Is", from the musical *You're a Good Man Charlie Brown.* (YouTube has several versions.)

a) Ask kids what makes them happy (for example, learning to whistle or climbing a tree).

b) Use the ideas in the song to brainstorm a longer list of activities that make kids happy that are age appropriate. Older kids will have different ideas than are presented in this song: for example, putting up the Christmas tree, going window shopping with a friend, or using Skype to stay in touch on the Internet with friends who are far away.

c) Check off ideas that work for each child.

d) Ask kids to write their own lyrics and sing the new lines to the same tune.

Activity Songs, Books, Movies & TV

Start this activity by discussing your favourite happy songs, books, movies and TV shows. Include ones that give you a good vibe and lift your mood.

Kids could create a chart with a section for each media to start to record their own lists.
This activity could be a resolution in their Happiness Project.

Activity — My Happiness List

"I may not be perfect but parts of me are excellent." —Ashleigh Brilliant, artist and writer

As a result of what you've learned from your resolutions over your twenty-one day trial periods, develop a list of actions you can take that truly make you happy. We will call this Your Happiness List. (Rubin called these actions her Twelve Commandments.) This list will guide your future behaviour.

Decide on your final Happiness List of what makes you happy and record it on a file card or smaller piece of paper you can keep with you or find quickly when you need it. You could also open a computer file to store the information.

Put your Happiness List on a message on the screensaver of your computer, tablet or cell phone.

You could share the list with your parents or a good friend to make a commitment to using this list on a regular basis.

As time goes on, you will want to update the list and add or delete ideas.

Gathering It Together

Kids may want to use a scrapbook or binder to store their work from different activities all in one place for future reference.

It's a good idea to go back to these activities to remind ourselves as time goes by to stay connected with the content and keep applying the activities.

Activity All On One Page

In addition to creating a scrapbook or binder, making a one-page summary will be useful for parents, teachers and kids to see the world of a child from the child's point of view. Use these categories:

a) My signature strengths summary of what I am good at
b) My Happiness List
c) What people like about me (from family and friends)
d) What's important to me
e) How adults can support me
f) A photo of me

—adapted from Helen Sanderson's *One Page Profile*

When Kids Don't Feel Happy

It's natural for kids to experience a wide range of feelings. No one feels happy all the time. All feelings are acceptable and valid. It is important to get support around more challenging feelings. No one can prevent "stuff" from happening. *Kids Help Phone* in Canada says that "(e)very young person will experience disappointment and sadness. What's important is how they deal with these powerful feelings." Often the only way to get past a troublesome difficult situation is to just go through it. Having someone for help and support can make all the difference.

"Life isn't about waiting for the storm to pass. It's about learning how to dance in the rain." —Source Unknown

Our Reactions Vary

Emotions are actually signals sent throughout the body from the brain that result in feelings. We need them to survive. Negative emotions keep us away from harm. Positive emotions give us energy and tell us that everything is okay.

If feelings last for a long time, they are called moods.

Sometimes, the feeling is short lived, and we snap out of it. It's like a dark cloud that passes over us—worrisome at the time, and then quickly gone. For some people, a good night's rest, a bit of time or a good cry helps them calm down. When any emotion become intense and reaches a peak, it is difficult to be logical and see things clearly. It helps to have a plan to deal with these times.

There are ultimately three routes to take when faced with challenging feelings:

a) Give in to the emotions and get "stuck" in them.
b) Hope that the problem will go away.
c) Tackle the problem with a positive outlook and belief that it will get better. Move into the emotions and get support if necessary.

The third route may seem more problematic, but it will pay off in the long run. It takes practice and determination to choose to go this way. It involves listening to and trusting emotions and the feelings they create.

Here are five easy-to-remember steps kids can take when faced with intense emotions. They could use these strategies when situations occur that they need to talk with a friend or an adult about. Sometimes, it's easier to share in a letter first before talking to someone.

1. What is really going on? Take a breath, try to be calm and clarify the facts.
2. How do I feel right now? Decide if the reaction is appropriate or an over-reaction.
3. Who can help me with this? Take a chance and trust a person who could help.
4. Is there anything that is beyond my control? Focus on what you can control.
5. What should I do first? Doing something is better than doing nothing.

> *"In a class of thirty students, six may be struggling with a mental-health problem or disorder. Most likely, only one in six will be receiving treatment."*
> —Melodie McCullough, "Support for Healthy Minds", *Professionally Speaking*, December, 2010

Mental Health Issues

Think of mental illness just as you would any other illness that will get worse if it isn't treated. Depression is a very common illness that can be treated with medication, counselling or both. *Kids Help Phone's* Mental Health Tip Sheet indicates that providing mental health education and facts isn't sufficient to break through the fear and stigma; while 75 percent of youth show good general knowledge of mental health issues, only 50 percent would consider reaching out if they were struggling with intense feelings. As one child said: "There's no one out there I trust enough to tell and I don't want to seem like a stupid kid." *Kids Help Phone* is both a telephone line and an information-packed website for kids and teens. *Kids Help Phone* offers free, 24/7, anonymous and confidential professional counselilng over the phone and online. It is available to young people all over Canada in both English and French. At *Kids Help Phone*, no problem is too big or too small—young people can contact them with any type of mental or emotional health concern, such as depression, or about other things too, like family, friends and dating relationships, or things going on at home or at school. A service like *Kids Help Phone* could be the very first way of reaching out for help.

"It is fear of rejection from friends and family, and the worries over confidentiality that are affecting children's willingness to seek help."
—*Kids Help Phone* Fact Sheet

If feelings of sadness last for more than a couple of weeks, it may be a depression. Sadness and depression aren't the same. Talking with a family doctor can help with a diagnosis of depression. *Kids Help Phone* counsellors identify the following as some of the most common signs of mental or emotional distress in young people:

- negative thoughts or feelings
- feelings of helplessness or hopelessness
- sad or "down" feelings
- a sudden drop in school grades
- sudden risk-taking
- a change in appetite or sleep patterns
- aggressive or disruptive behaviour

"Depression can be caused by bodily, psychological and environmental factors, or a combination of all three. Sometimes, depression can be genetic, which means that if someone in your family has had depression problems you may be more prone to developing it." —Kids Help Phone website

- withdrawal from friends or family
- loss of interest in hobbies
- unusual tiredness
- use of alcohol or drugs to cope with moods
- talking about death or suicide

Remove the Barriers and Start the Conversations

I urge teachers, parents—and kids themselves—to be sensitive to the emotions of kids around them in their family, class or community. Watch for kids who never seem to laugh. Try to find out more about them and start a relationship. Some may come from homes where they are taught to act "maturely". Some come from homes where there is no laughter. Some may be abused or bullied. Some may have eating disorders or have harmed themselves. Each one has his or her own story.

Let kids you are concerned about know they can talk with you about anything. Listen to what they have to say. Help them to feel more in control of their feelings instead of being controlled by them. You can help kids connect with support services in the community that they can trust.

It is worth repeating the following message: Don't expect the activities in this book to cheer up a child with depression who needs urgent attention. Find more appropriate means and professional help in a crisis. Principals and assistant principals, special education workers, guidance counsellors, teachers, doctors, and church leaders may be able to assist you with behaviour beyond the scope of this book.

If you're a teacher, respectfully facilitate access to other sources of help. You can help kids connect with support services in the community that they can trust. *Kids Help Phone* is a valuable resource. In a crisis, if there doesn't seem to be any other option, go with the child to the emergency ward at the hospital and seek help there. It's always okay to ask for help.

Some families regularly set aside a time to clear the air and talk about what's happening in general. They often find out there's more going on than they thought there was.

Reach Out For Help

Kids need to deal with their feelings and talk about them with trusted friends and adults in order to understand them.

Following is a list of phone numbers kids can use in different countries to reach out and get help. Adults could have this information handy when they are uncertain what to do to help a child. It never hurts to ask for help.

Canada—1-800-668-6868—*Kids Help Phone,* **Website www.KidsHelpPhone.ca** KHP is a cool place for kids to call if they want to talk about a problem. It's available online or on the phone. Trained counsellors are always there ready to listen 24/7 with nonjudgmental free counselling and information. It's anonymous and confidential. No problem is too big or too small—if it's important to you, it's important to them. They also have an information-packed website: www.KidsHelpPhone.ca

USA and Canada—National Child Abuse Hotline—
1-800-4-A-CHILD or 1-800-422-4453. Kids can call the Child Abuse Hotline any time if they are being abused or their parents aren't looking after them properly. What they say on the Child Abuse Hotline will be kept private.

UK—Emergency 999

UK—Childline 0800 1111 Kids can call Childline any time if they are having any kind of problem, or are just upset. Kids should think about calling them if they are being abused, bullied, or their parents aren't looking after them properly. What kids say on Childline will be kept private.

Australia—Emergency 000 Australia—Kids Help Line 1-800-55-1800
Kids can call the Kids Help Line any time. They can call about any kind of problems: drug and alcohol, relationships, abuse, or mental health issues such as depression or anxiety. What they say on Kid's Help Line will be kept private.

New Zealand—Emergency 111 KIDSLINE 0800-543-754
Kids can call KidsLine between 4—6pm weekdays. What they say on Kid's Help Line will be kept private.

European Union Countries—Emergency 112

Child Helpline International
If your country is not listed, look up your country on Child Helpline International. Sixty-one countries have helplines for children.

Pleasant and Unpleasant Feelings

It's normal to experience a wide range of emotions in life. Each emotion has a purpose and a meaning for us when it occurs at the right time and in the right amount. Rather than judging feelings as either positive and negative, or good and bad, it's more productive to reframe them as pleasant and unpleasant (challenging) for us in different situations. All emotions have a positive value.

It may come as a surprise to count the number of feelings we find unpleasant and compare that list to feelings that we do like and enjoy. In our vocabulary for our range of feelings, there are far more unpleasant words. (This is called a "negativity bias" in the research.) So we need to concentrate on the pleasant emotions in our lives that calm and soothe us and try to reduce the unpleasant. Researcher Barbara Frederickson and her colleagues at the University of California focus on "positivity". They emphasize that we need to aim for three times more positive or pleasant emotional experiences to try to balance the negativity that surround us.

Of specific concern are the feelings out of the normal range that are signs of a mental health concern.

Activity: Coping in Healthy Ways

Make two lists of strategies people use when they aren't happy in order to cope and feel better. One list is for positive, healthy ways and the other is for unhealthy ways. See how long you can make the two lists. For example, a healthy way to cope would be to talk to someone about what's happening. Getting drunk would be an unhealthy way to cope.

Discuss which methods are shortcuts to feeling better that don't last in the long run.

Review Activities in Part One

Kids have already experienced some key activities in this book to get them moving in a positive direction. Reviewing these activities may help a child reset negative feelings.

1. Their Happiness Line Survey

2. Their Awesome List
3. Their Signature Strengths Survey
4. Their Happiness Project and Happiness List

"I think I needed to remind myself there were bright spots in the darkness. I think I needed a place where I could smile at the little things we all smile silently at throughout our days . . . I'm also reminded of the joy and relief of letting awesome things cheer me up while I struggled to keep moving."
—Pasricha. 2011, p.378

Distract Yourself From the Problem

Here are some suggestions to experiment with to distract you from the problem and bring about greater calm and happiness.

A) Laugh

As the old saying goes, "A good laugh can banish a thousand worries". Take your mind off the problem for a while with a favourite comedy TV show. Watch a hilarious movie. Hang out with a funny friend. Even the newspaper comics can make you laugh.

> *"Kids who are able to laugh at the funny side of life can be described as internally happy."*
> —Louis Franzini

Try looking at your situation through a funny lens. I met a group of young adults in Toronto who did just that when I was a keynote speaker at a conference focusing on well-being. I partnered my speech with a group called Stand-Up For Comedy and their teacher Michael Cole, aka "The Humour Coach". They were graduates of a sixteen week program called *Laughing Like Crazy* sponsored by the Mood Disorders Association of Ontario. The program combines the benefits of peer support with the social, physical and emotional benefits of laughter.

Four brave participants in the program shared their own stand-up comedy routine with the audience based on their experiences with mental health issues and the mental health system. They even conquered their fears of speaking in public. We learned about the life issues these performers were dealing with such as alcoholism, depression, compulsive eating, and bipolar disorder. One had tried to commit suicide. After their routines, audience members asked them what they had gained from being in the program. I vividly remember one woman revealing that it had saved her life. Many *Laughing Like Crazy* graduates have returned to work, finished school, earned promotions and discovered creative passions. Most of all, they told stories about how they had healed, strengthened and developed their relationships with family and friends.

Charlie Chaplin said "Comedy is two opposite ideas that collide".

That couldn't be more true of mental health issues and stand-up comedy!

While this is a program for young adults, it is included here to emphasize the benefits of laughter when faced with problems —even life-threatening ones. One of their sayings is: "By laughing at our differences we can rise above them." There are many applications of this program to the lives of children.

Refer to Parts Two and Three to learn more about laughter, humour and comedy.

B) Relax

Experiment with various relaxation techniques and see what works for you.

- deep breathing
- yoga or dance
- music
- working out in the gym
- walking
- building something

> *"The last of human freedoms—the ability to choose our attitude in a given set of circumstances."* —Victor Frankl, a Jewish psychiatrist in Vienna, who suffered greatly during the Holocaust

C) Think Positive

Optimistic thinking is the tendency to expect the best in life and to believe that things will work out well in the future. It is the opposite of pessimism. Optimism helps us to feel a sense of control in a difficult situation. It pushes out the negative feelings. It helps us to find the energy to keep searching for a workable solution and to believe something can be done about a bad situation. It's the type of thinking in the classic children's book *The Little Engine That Could,* about a little train that had a huge mountain to climb that kept telling itself "I Think I Can" until it became "I Know I Can."

- Give yourself a pep talk.
- Write down a positive affirmation that builds confidence. For example, "We can do this together". or, "I have done this before". Say it out loud.
- Visualize your success.

Seligman believes that "it is impossible to sustain a negative mood in the presence of a large number of positive memories, expectations and beliefs, and it is impossible to sustain a positive mood in the presence of a large number of negative thoughts. Positive thoughts can outweigh negative ones."

He suggests to parents that they ask their kids two questions at the dinner table or bedtime:

1. What did you like doing today?
2. Did anything bad or sad happen today?

Compare the two lists to get an overall feeling for how the day went for each child. He suggests then adding the question: "What are you looking forward to tomorrow?" This is the optimistic at work.

We need to learn to give up hope for having a perfect past. What happened yesterday cannot be changed. Today is a gift. That's why we call it the "present". We are always learning more about ourselves—life is a work in progress. No one is perfect. Everyone has problems to deal with. It's how we deal with our problems that makes the difference.

Implementation Ideas: Put On a Happy Face

Testing the Water

Reflect on your range on the Happiness Line.

Reflect on the range of your kids and close friends.

Start to observe facial expressions and body language.

Listen to your language—is it happy or sad talk?

Think about how you normally react when you don't feel happy.

Getting Your Feet Wet

Try to move yourself to your upper range on the Happiness Line.

Start your own Awesome List to be more aware of little things that make you happy.

Consider the results when you take the Twenty-Four Strengths survey online.

Start conversations to reach out and help someone.

Jumping in the Deep End

Start your own Happiness Project.

Develop your own Happiness List and use it regularly.

Make happiness , positive psychology and well-being the theme for a course, or even for the whole school.

Ask one or two trusted friends or family members to give you regular feedback on your moods.

Teach the key messages to someone else and pay it forward.

Dig into the resources to learn more.

What implementation ideas would you add?

Resources on Happiness and Other Emotions

Books

Achor, Shawn. (2010). *The Happiness Advantage: The Seven Principles of Positive Psychology That Fuel Success and Performance at Work*. New York, NY: Crown Business.

Cain, Janan. (2000) *The Way I Feel.* Seattle, WA: Parenting Press, Inc.

Csikszentmihalyi, Mihaly. (2002). *Flow: The Classic Work on How to Achieve Happiness.* London: Rider Books.

Curtis, Jamie Lee. (1998). *Today I Feel Silly & Other Moods That Make My Day.* New York, NY: HarperCollins.

Dalai Lama. (2010). *The Essence of Happiness: A Guidebook for Living.* New York, NY: Riverhead.

Davies, R. (1977). Is it no. One-half of Robertson Davies. New York: Viking.

Diener, Ed and Robert. (2008). *Happiness: Unlocking the Mysteries of Psychological Wealth.* Walden, Ma: Blackwell Publishing.

Dr. Seuss. (1996). *My Many Colored Days.* New York, NY: Knopf Doubleday (Random House).

Elffers, Joost and Freymann Saxton. (1999). *How Are You Peeling?: Foods With Moods.* New York, NY: Arthur A. Levine Books.

Fordyce, Michael. *Social Indicators Research.* 20, 355-381. Jan. 2006.

Fredrickson, Barbara. (2009) *Positivity.* New York, NY: Crown.

Gilbert, Daniel. (2006) *Stumbling on Happiness.* New York, NY: Knopf.

Happiness *Harvard Business Review* (Jan-Feb 2012).

Holden, Robert. (2007) *Happiness Now! Timeless Wisdom for Feeling Good Fast.* Carlsbad, Ca: Hay House, Inc.

Holmes, Jessica. (2010) *I Love Your Laugh: Finding the Light in My Screwball Life*. Toronto, On: McClelland & Stewart.

Huebner, Dawn. (2005). *What To Do When You Worry Too Much: A kid's guide to overcoming anxiety*. Washington, DC: American Psychological Association.

Johnson, Helen. "Counteracting Performativity in Schools: the Case for Laughter As a Qualitative and Redemptive Indicator." *International Journal of Children's Spirituality*. Vol. 10, No. 1, April 2005, pp. 81-96.

Klein, Allen. (1989) *The Healing Power of Humor: Techniques for Getting through Loss, Setbacks, Disappointments, Difficulties, Trials, Tribulations, and All That Not-So-Funny Stuff*. New York, NY: Penguin Putnam Inc.

Klein, Allen. (2011). *Learning to Laugh When You Feel Like Crying: Embracing Life After Loss*. Norwood, NJ: Goodman Beck.

Lamia, Mary. (2011). *Understanding Myself: A kid's guide to intense emotions and strong feelings*. Washington, DC: American Psychological Association.

LaRoche, Loretta. (1996). *Happy Talk: Fun Ways to Talk to Yourself*. The Humor Potential.

Pasricha, Neil. (2011) *The Book of (Even More) Awesome*. New York, NY: Penguin.

Pasricha, Neil. (2010) *The Book of Awesome*. New York, NY: Putnam.

Rubin, Gretchen. (2012) *Happier at Home: Kiss More, Jump More, Abandon a Project, Read Samuel Johnson, and My Other Experiments in the Practice of Life*. New York, NY: Random House Inc.

Rubin, Gretchen. (2009) *The Happiness Project: Or Why I Spent a Year Trying to Sing in the Morning, Clean My Closets, Fight Right, Read Aristotle, and Generally Have More Fun*. New York, NY: Harper.

Seligman, Martin. (2011). *Flourish: A Visionary Understanding of Happiness and Well-Being.* New York, NY: Free Press.

Seligman, Martin. (2002) *Authentic Happiness: Using the New Positive Psychology to Realize Your Potential for Lasting Fulfillment.* New York, NY: Free Press.

Shadyac, Tom. Director. (2011) *I AM* [Film], USA, Shady Acres Entertainment.

Sher, Barbara. (2002). *Spirit Games: 300 Fun Activities That Bring Children Comfort and Joy.* New York, NY: John Wiley & Sons, Inc.

Stephenson, Susan and Thibault, Paul. (2006). *Laughing Matters!.* Bloomington, IN: Solution Tree Press.

Stronach, Enid. (2011). *Soldier On – Overcoming Grief by Living Through It.* High Point, NC: TRI Publishing Co.

Websites

Action for Happiness—**www.actionforhappiness.org**

Canadian Mental Health Association—**www.cmha.ca**

Canadian Positive Psychology Association—

www.positivepsychologycanada.com

Center for Positive Psychology, UPEN—**www.ppc.sas.upenn.edu**

Centre for Addiction and Mental Health (resources and information)

—**www.camh.net**

Greater Good Science Centre—**www.greatergood.berkley.edu**

Happy—**www.TheHappyMovie.com**

Note: The Educational Edition of the Happy film was released in the fall 2012. It includes downloadable instructor's guides for grades 6–12 and higher, closed captioning, 30 minutes of bonus features and 9 subtitle languages.

Helen Sanderson's One Page Profiles—

www.helensandersonassociates.co.uk

Huffington Post Good News—**www.huffingtonpost.com/good-news**

I Am documentary—**www.iamthedoc.com**

Mood Disorders Association—**www.mood disorders.ca**

Motherlode (parenting blog)—**www.parenting.blogs.nytimes.com**

Positive Psychology News Daily—**www.positivepsychologynews.com**

Psychology Today Blogs: Find happiness-related blogs—**www.psychologytoday.com/blog/index**

The Happiness Initiative—**www.happycounts.org**

The Happiness Project—**www.happinessproject.com**

VIA Institute on Character—**www.viacharacter.org**

Part Two

LOL—Laughing Out Loud

"Among those whom I like I can find no common denominator, but among those that I love, I can: all of them make me laugh."—W.H. Auden

---

LOL is an emoticon for "laughing out loud" or "laugh out loud". Another version of it is ROFL for "rolling on the floor laughing". A friend of mine, Val, originally thought it meant "Lots of Love", and that misinterpretation made for funny emails with her son Kyle. One time he sent Val an email about a minor car accident he'd had, and she responded: "Hope you didn't gct any bumps or strained muscles. LOL, Mom." His response was: "I am Laughing Out Loud at your email response."

To look after our health we all need to eat more fibre, drink more water, eat less sugar and salt—and laugh more. Why do you think laughter is good for our physical health? Do you think laughter can ease tensions in sad and difficult situations? Do you need to have a good sense of humour to laugh? Parents and teachers need to teach kids more about laughter and make it a daily practice in their own lives.

Laughter researcher Robert Provine says that we laugh or smile when we feel the emotion of mirth. He likens "mirth" to a pleasurable feeling closely related to glee, hilarity, joy or exhilaration—all at the upper part of the Happiness Line.

Part Two focuses on laughter that happens spontaneously either by yourself but more commonly with other people.

a) A Laughter Ladder to use as a graphic organizer

b) Twenty-one laughter benefits for kids
c) Laughter Clubs for kids
d) Laughter organizations dedicated to help

Spontaneous Laughter in Conversations

In their various studies on sources of humour, Canadian researchers Rod Martin and Nicholas Kuiper report that:

- Only 11 percent of daily laughter comes from jokes.
- Another 17 percent comes from the media.
- A whopping 72 percent comes from interactions with other people in the forms of comments or stories.

—Martin, 2007 p.12

In other words, the majority of our humour in our social relationships with others (friends, family, classmates, siblings, spouses, relatives, work colleagues) is spontaneous. These comments can pop out when you're talking in person or on the phone, or when you're writing a letter, an email, a text message or a tweet.

This statistic could lead to many interesting discussions with children about the social value of having meaningful relationships with people so we can laugh—and also cry when we need to—together. To be happy and find the humour in life, we need connections to other people.

"Children and adults may appreciate the same expressions of humor. . . .but what you should understand is that it is often the subject of the humor and the way it is presented that will strike people of different intellectual levels and experiences as funny."
—Franzini, p.12

Children Love to Laugh

Children living in safe environments with enough food and a roof over their heads tend to spend their days smiling, grinning and chuckling—they're kids after all. It would be hard to count all their laughs. Children laugh with their whole body. In fact, children who are born deaf and blind start laughing and smiling even though they can't learn this from others by hearing them or seeing them. On the other hand, kids who grow up in environments where they are hungry or feel unsafe don't spend much time laughing.

Most adults need to give themselves permission to laugh more often and wake up their inner child. As an adult, how many laughs per day (LPDs) do you think you have? It is often stated that adults laugh fifteen times a day compared to three to four hundred times a day for kids. There doesn't seem to be any scientific research for these numbers, although the general trend makes sense.

Activity: Three Basic Sounds of Laughter

Three basic sounds are the origins of all laughs. Their energy comes from various parts of the body. All three are based on an H sound—huffing it out.

- Hee-Hee-Hee: This is a sound from your head and mouth.
- Ha-Ha-Ha: This is the sound from your chest or heart area.
- Ho-Ho-Ho: This is the sound from your belly or stomach, like the one Santa Claus makes.

All laughter is a combination of these three sounds. Have kids practise them as whispers at first, with a signal to get louder. Practise along with them.

The Ladder of Laughter

There are so many types of laughs, and it's fun to sort them out. This Ladder of Laughter is meant to show the huge range of the types of laughter. They all begin and end with a smile.

crying with laughter

full belly laughs

big, deep laughs or guffaws

snorts

chuckles

giggles

snickers

wider smiles or grins

slight smiles

twinkles in the eye

no smiles

Note: The DVD ***Good Morning Miss Toliver*** is an excellent resource for teachers that portrays a multitude of ways she uses practical activities, positive reinforcement and a genuine sense of humour and fun to connect with her middle school students and increase their achievement—and she teaches mathematics in East Harlem. The comments from the students in Kay Toliver's class are powerful and loving. Toliver was the recipient of the prestigious Peabody Award in 1993.

Activity: More Sounds of Laughter

Humans make distinctive sounds and movements when they laugh. The sound of laughter is made by air passing over vibrating vocal cords in the throat. Someone observing laughter for the first time would hear loud barking-like noises and possibly detect faster breathing, an open mouth and various facial expressions, the throwing of the head back and perhaps rocking back and forth. It's often hard for people to keep breathing when they laugh really hard. Sometimes their face will feel warmer and they may tear up.

Watch and listen to the clip *A Couple of Laughs* on YouTube to get an idea of different laughs. Take a look at examples of gibberish as well.

If you are a teacher, listen to the sounds of laughter in your classroom and out in the playground. Listen to the sounds of laughter on buses and subways. Listen to sounds of laughter with people at home. Try placing the laughs on the Laughter Ladder.

Can you find a friend or family member in a crowded room just by hearing his or her laugh? Has this ever happened to you?

How does YOUR real laugh sound like? Have you ever heard yourself on a recording or a DVD?

"Laughter—that is something very sacred, especially for us Indians."
—John (Fire) Lame Deer, Rosebud Lakota

Activity The Laughing Symphony

One person takes on the role of a symphony conductor and takes the group members up and down the Laughter Ladder making the sounds and movements at each step. Once everyone gets the "hang of it", vary the sequence of steps. The conductor could also instruct some individuals to laugh at various steps and be silent while others laugh.

Contagious Laughter

Laughter spreads quickly from person to person and can be contagious. Often when we hear laughter, we smile and may even start laughing. Here are two examples.

The Laughter Video, produced by "Jollytologist" Allen Klein, has 15 minutes of continuous and contagious hee-haws and guffaws. Just watching it for a few minutes makes viewers start laughing at the wide variety of types of laughs.

Laughology, by Canadian filmmaker and "laughologist" Albert Nerenberg, is a 2009 documentary film about the contagiousness of human laughter. It is the first feature-length documentary about laughter. In the film we are introduced to Doug Collins, who was part of a live Comedy Barn TV show in Tennessee and easily won the contest for the man with the most contagious laugh. (You can also catch Doug Collins on YouTube and there is an app called The Laughman.)

The Skype Laughter Chain on YouTube is an intriguing collection of people of all ages laughing and the reactions of others as they watch each laugher.

Smiles Turn Frowns Upside Down

"The whole art of life is knowing how to transform anxiety into laughter."
—Alan Watts

As we saw on the Laughter Ladder, all laughs begin and end with a smile. Fifteen different muscles move in your face to create a smile. Smiling is said to make us look younger. In contrast, it takes forty-three muscles to frown. Research shows that the smile is the most easily detected facial expression of all. It can be accurately perceived from a distance of one hundred meters.

There are two types of smiles based on how genuine they are. A real, honest, mirthful smile is called a Duchenne smile (after its discoverer Guillaume Duchenne, a French neurologist). You can identify this one mainly by looking at the eyes and laugh lines around them and the upturned corners of the mouth. The person is smiling in a friendly way. A fake smile is called the Pan American smile. It is emotionless and intended to hide one's true feelings (named after airline flight attendants who are forced to smile for passengers).

Note: For a powerful presentation on The Hidden Power of Smiling, go to www.tedtalks.com featuring Ron Gutman.

Revisit the Feelings and Faces Photo Search activity from Part One and examine the smiles in the photos you found. Are they Duchenne or Pan American smiles? Is it easier to judge real smiles from a photograph or in person?

All of the activities in your Awesome List and Happiness List will bring smiles to your face. When you are using your signature strengths, you will surely be smiling too.

Smiling is contagious. You catch it like the flu.
When someone smiled at me today, I started smiling too.
I passed around the corner, and someone saw my grin;
When he smiled, I realized I'd passed it on to him.
I thought about that smile, then I realized its worth.
A single smile, just like mine, could travel round the earth.
So if you feel a smile begin, don't leave it undetected
Let's start an epidemic quick and get the world infected.
—Source Anonymous

Take a Scientific Look at Laughter

Gelos was the Greek god of laughter.
Gelotology is the science of laughter (pronounced gee-lo-*tahl*-o-gee)
A gelotologist is a professional laughter expert.

For centuries people instinctively knew that laughter was a good thing. Major advances were made in the twentieth century, and the pioneers in this field—the first gelotologists— are worthy of note. In 1964, Dr. William Fry realized that the study of laughter could indeed be a science and got the ball rolling at Stanford University as a researcher into the psychology of laughter. He has since become a leading expert on humour and health.

Joel Goodman is an expert on the positive power of humour and creativity. He founded The HUMOR Project in 1977.
In his bestselling book *Anatomy of an Illness* (1979), Norman Cousins, an American magazine editor, focused the discussion of humour on pain relief. Cousins was diagnosed in the early 1960s with a very painful form of arthritis, with a slim chance of recovery. He combined massive doses of vitamin C with watching television comedies and reading joke books. His goal

was to replace negative, unpleasant emotions with ones that were pleasant and positive. His reports that ten minutes of laughter led to two hours free of pain were astounding. His book led Dr. Lee Berk to continue the groundbreaking research on humour at Loma Linda University in California.

Originating in ancient India, yoga has been practised for hundreds of years. In 1995, Dr. Madan Kataria decided to start a laughter club in Bombay (Mumbai), India, with the goal of helping people feel happier in a playful group setting. He first met with five people in a public park, and they started out telling jokes and stories, but when their repertoire ran out, he looked for another source of laughter. Kataria had read Cousins's book and Berk's original research results and was surprised to discover that "the body cannot differentiate between real and simulated laughter. . . If one cannot laugh, one could pretend to laugh" (Kataria, p. 15). He began to ask his followers to act out laughter without jokes for a few minutes, and the popularity of his new form of laughter yoga grew.

Dr. Rod Martin of the University of Western Ontario, in Canada, continues the field of research on the psychology of humour. His 2007 book *The Psychology of Humor: an integrative approach* provides a detailed reference book on the subject.

The World Laughter Tour

My introduction to Laughter Clubs was through Steve Wilson and the **World Laughter Tour** based in Columbus, Ohio. I became a Certified Laughter Leader or CLL in 2006 (or "certifiable" as my husband Tom says) and have led many laughter sessions since then for a wide variety of educational, corporate and community groups.

Steve Wilson, an American psychologist specializing in mental health and humour since 1964 and a self-proclaimed 'Joyologist,' started the **World Laughter Tour** and continues to be the inspiration and genius behind this wonderfully successful organization that is leading the laughter movement. Steve had an opportunity to share his beliefs with Dr. Madan Kataria in 1999 when, joined by Karen Buxman, a colleague, nurse and speaker, they toured multiple cities together.

Since then, the diverse recipients of training from the **World Laughter Tour** have included parents, nurses, teachers, psychologists, social workers, marriage and family counsellors, nuns, volunteers, consultants and military personnel and their families.

Steve Wilson and his **World Laughter Tour** have extended the application of therapeutic laughter in unique ways:

- Two-day certification sessions with more than six thousand Certified Laughter Leaders (CLLs) in the USA, Canada and Mexico
- Formation of hundreds of Laughter Club programs for schools including ground-breaking, intergenerational clubs that bring school children to seniors' residences to laugh together
- Extensive materials, resources, support and networking
- Development of the *Laughter Arts and Sciences Foundation (LASF)* to provide scholarships and promote research
- Establishment of college-affiliated, accredited training
- Formation of a *National Humor Month* including "Funny Literacy"activities (see Part Three)
- Formation of a Professional Advisory Committee

The World Laughter Tour motto is: " **Laughter is contagious, so let's start an epidemic."**

Its mission is: **"Together we can lead the world to health, happiness and peace through laughter."**

Sue Stephenson
and Steve Wilson
November 2012

Good-Hearted Living

By Steve Wilson, © 2001-2012 All Rights Reserved
—Used with permission from Steve Wilson

WORLD LAUGHTER TOUR tm
Think Globally, Laugh Locally

Steve Wilson has developed a collection of daily practices called **Good-Hearted Living** for each day of the week that, in combination, have a special way of delivering laughter and happiness and preventing what he calls "hardening of the attitudes".

The ideas are easy and fun. Begin with mindfulness: remember what practice the day is for. Each day, whenever you see an opportunity, take some action to do the practice for that day. Just do it! Your actions will become habits, and the habits will become the natural and positive way of life for you. Do this for as little as five minutes every day. Soon you will be amazed to find that you laugh more, are more cheerful and optimistic and feel better in general.

Teachers could include this in their morning organization along with the weather and other announcements.

Good-Hearted Living

By Steve Wilson, © 2001-2012 All Rights Reserved
—Used with permission from Steve Wilson

Mondays are for compliments, so **Say Nice Things to Yourself and Other People** instead of criticizing and judging others.

Tuesdays are for flexibility, so **Try Doing Some New Things in a New Way** instead of being stubborn and stuck in a rut.

Wednesdays are for an attitude of gratitude, so **Be Glad for What You Have** instead of wanting things you don't have.

Thursdays are for kindness, so **Be Kind to Others** instead of being mean or hurtful.

Fridays are for forgiveness, so **Forgive Others** instead of being angry and holding a grudge.

AND
Weekends are for "chocolate". Literally, remember to eat some chocolate or any other favourite food. Metaphorically, this means **Relax and Have Fun!**

Another Look at Gratitude

It's easy to forget everything we have to be grateful for when we are caught up in the stresses of day-to-day living. Steve Wilson once told me: "There's an old saying that if you've forgotten the language of gratitude, you'll never be on speaking terms with happiness."

Melody Beattie, author of *Co-Dependent No More*, put it this way: "Gratitude unlocks the fullness of life. It turns what we have into enough and more. It turns denial into acceptance, chaos into order, confusion into clarity. It can turn a meal into a feast, a house into a home, a stranger into a friend. Gratitude makes sense of our past, brings peace for today, and creates a vision for tomorrow."

Try keeping a daily gratitude journal, either in the morning or before you go to bed, to record three things you are grateful for in your life.

Watch the *Gratitude Dance* on YouTube and add it to your repertoire.

Laughter Clubs for Adults

A typical thirty-to-sixty minute Laughter Club for adults follows this format:

- An invitation to participate and interact in a childlike, playful manner
- Some information about the benefits of laughter and the difference between laughing this way as compared to laughing at jokes and comedy
- Descriptions and demonstrations of various laughter exercises or laughs that participants then try for a minute or two
- A clapping signal from the leader while saying Ho Ho Ha Ha Ha used to draw each exercise to a close
- Stretching and breathing breaks inserted between laughs
- Opportunities for creative expression and comments from the leader and the participants suited to the group
- A few moments of relaxation at the end of the session

All participants need to be careful not to hurt themselves or others when they are laughing. Laughter requires that people breathe deeply and use their abdominal muscles. People who have had abdominal surgery or have other physical limitations need to adjust the physicality and take it very easy. People with these medical conditions need to be more cautious: a hernia, hemorrhoids, pregnancy, heart disease with chest pain, severe colds, flu or a persistent cough. If there is any doubt at all, consult a doctor before participating.

Laughter Clubs for Kids

In schools, homes or other settings, five to ten minutes is a good way to start out with laughter exercises. Aim for a maximum of thirty minutes to keep the attention of younger children. Laughing involves a lot more breathing, so make sure kids stay hydrated. Children have no trouble laughing, especially when they are in a group. These exercises work well with elementary as well as high school students with the right introduction and leader.

Teachers and staff should experience this approach before a laughter leader works with students. Laughter sessions of five to ten minutes work well at school assemblies to energize students. Students can stand to do the laughs and move around in their places. In a classroom, kids could be led through five minutes of laughter exercises at the beginning or end of the day. It is especially beneficial to help kids relax before a test or examination.

Here are some additional suggestions for Laughter Clubs for kids:

- Have children sit in chairs or at desks for the first few sessions.
- Ask them to then try standing in a circle or sitting on benches or on a carpet, or take them outside.
- Refer to the Laughing Ladder.
- Review the Safe Laughter Guidelines (see following).
- Tell them laughter is fun and makes us feel good.
- Mention the anatomy of the diaphragm, vocal cords and lungs.

- When they have some experience, have them take turns at being a leader.
- To quickly draw the attention back, use a signal such as raising your hand, squeezing a bicycle horn or clapping.
- Include the *Good Hearted Living Daily Practices.*
- Cool down with some affirmations like "I love to laugh. I love catching a laugh. Laughter makes me feel good".
- End with applause for having such a great time laughing.

Intergenerational Laughter Clubs

An exciting application of laughter clubs for kids was the brainchild of two Certified Laughter Leaders and a teacher in Canton Ohio—Peggy Stabholtz, CLL and counsellor; Nancy Engle, CLL and Director of Social Services, Bethany Nursing Home; and Debbie Davidson, teacher at Walker Elementary School. Since 1999, they have been bringing school children to a seniors' residence for a combined, intergenerational laughter club with visible results for all of the participants—no matter what their age. Everyone benefits from the laughter, and new relationships are formed across the ages. Kids develop more caring and respect for the seniors, and the seniors pick up some of the youthful vitality from the kids.

Nancy, Peggy and Debbie suggest bringing the two groups together once or twice to establish a relationship before the first laughter club. After that, monthly sessions would be ideal. The families and staff also benefit by getting involved themselves.

If you would like to learn more about this concept, contact Steve Wilson at www.worldlaughtertour.com or 1-800-NOW-LAFF (669-5233).

Safe Laughter Guidelines

Here are some guidelines to consider to make laughing safe and fun.

1. The only person you can safely laugh at is yourself.
2. Laugh WITH other people, not AT them.
3. If everyone isn't laughing, it's not funny to someone.
4. If others are laughing AT someone else and making fun of them, try to gently step in and stop it.
5. Laughter is always a voluntary choice.
6. A sense of humour isn't necessary in order to laugh.
7. You cannot "die laughing", as the old saying goes.
8. It's easier to laugh with someone when you make eye contact.
9. Laughter means you are "in the moment".

Do you agree with each of these guidelines? Would you add any others? Involve kids in a process to develop their own list.

Activity — Try Some Laughter Exercises

You don't need to be a comedian or tell jokes to have your own laughter club—you only need to laugh and move. Here are a few laughter activities you can do alone, with a friend or in a group to have fun together. Be creative and make up your own laughs too.

These laughs stimulate energy:

1. **The Laughter Chant**—Say "*HO HO, HA HA HA*" and clap your hands with each word quietly or loudly. You can even add your own laugh to this chant.

2. **Wash-Your-Hands Laugh**—Giggle or laugh while pretending to wash hands for twenty seconds.

3. **Milkshake Laugh**—Pretend you are holding two big glasses and pour a thick milkshake back and forth from glass to glass while laughing, then take a "drink" and start again.

4. **Lion Laugh**—Put your hands up with your fingers stretched like claws. Open your mouth up really wide like a lion roaring, only laugh instead.

5. **Follow-the-Leader Laugh**—One person does a one-minute laugh and then others copy him or her, as in the Simon Says game. Rotate leaders throughout the group so everyone gets a chance to lead. Focus on facial expressions and body movements as well as different sounds and laughs.

6. **Roller Coaster Laugh**—People sit in chairs in a line and pretend to be on a roller coaster, giggling on the low parts and laughing as they go over the top.

7. **Penguin Laugh**—Walk around with your arms and feet like a penguin, laughing like one.

8. **Fan-out-On-the-Floor Laugh**—Lie on the ground with some friends and laugh. Can you feel the vibrations on the floor? Try laughing back-to-back with someone else and see what happens.

9. **Try-Not-to-Laugh Laugh** - Two people face each other without touching and one person tries to get the other person to laugh. The other person tries not to laugh for as long as he or she can.

10. **The Ha Ha Game**—The first person says "*HA*", the second person says "*HA HA*", the third person says "*HA HA HA*" and so on until everyone is laughing!

11. **High Tens**—Double the fun of a high five. In pairs, one person lifts both his hands up high and his partner responds with a double palm-on-palm smack. Try doing this laugh in slow motion. As people touch hands, they laugh.

12. **Beach Ball in the Air**—Everyone in the group is ready to receive the ball and keep it in the air. One child throws the beach ball to another child, escalating the level of laughter from the Laughter Ladder as the ball continues around the group. The goal is to touch the ball, involve everyone in the group and keep the ball in the air. Try this for five to ten consecutive catches and beach-ball laughs. If the ball hits the ground, start again. Everyone quickly learns to keep the ball off the floor and the ceiling. Many children will miss the ball or make a silly hit. Encourage them to laugh at themselves if this happens.

As kids get used to these laughs, you could add a new twist by introducing gibberish to them (making up new words in a nonsensical language).

These laughs have a calming effect:

1. **Silent Laugh**—Laugh without making any sounds, using facial expressions and body movements—for example lips sealed. (Think how helpful this would be in a discussion of when it's not okay to laugh out loud.)

2. **Pause Button**—The leader pretends to have a remote control and points it at people in the group and clicks to pause their laughter temporarily, and then clicks a second time to have them resume.

3. **Big Toothy Grin**—Make a big grin showing as many teeth as you can, including laughing with your eyes, without laughing out loud.

4. **Lower-Laughter Ladder**—Practise the quiet smiles and grins at the lower rungs of the Laughter Ladder.

5. **Ice-Cube-Down-the-Back Laugh**—Stand in pairs, pretend it's a hot day and drop a make-believe ice cube down your own back, laughing as it works its way down. As a cool-down, pretend the ice cube totally melts into a little puddle as participants quietly put their heads down on a table or "melt" on the floor.

After each laugh exercise, provide some time to reflect on and talk about how it felt. Kids may be able to suggest refinements for the next time.

A great way to introduce you to many laughs and see them in action is *The Laughter Club Song (with titles)* on YouTube. It is written by Jeffrey Briar, founder of the Laughter Yoga Institute. If you search under Jeffrey's name 'JoyfulGent,' you will also find about twenty YouTube clips that demonstrate a rich diversity of information he has created to share with others.

Simple Deep Breathing Techniques

As both a warm-up or after a laugh exercise, take a few deep breaths in and out from the belly so that you don't run out of air. Inhale while raising your arms and breathe in with the fresh air. Exhale with the stale air while lowering your arms. Do this a few times to regain normal breathing. Kids could imagine that their lungs are balloons, and that when they breathe in and out, they are blowing them up and then letting out the air. Go slowly, and gradually breathe more deeply. Anyone who feels dizzy should sit down and just breathe normally. Suggest these images as kids breathe deeply:

- Smelling snowflakes as they gently fall to the ground
- Smelling flowers in a garden
- Smelling popcorn in a movie theatre

Get Your Kids Laughing

What works in your family to get everyone giggling and playing together? Change routines for a laugh. For example, play the day backwards by wearing pajamas all day, eating hamburgers for breakfast and waffles for dinner. Watch a favourite comedy movie together. Put funny notes of encouragement in lunch bags or backpacks. Play funny board games together, such as **Apples to Apples, Pictionary, and Don't Make Me Laugh.**

Comedian and author Jessica Holmes uses the following technique anytime there is whining or a grumpy expression. She does an impression of whatever her kids are doing—times two. She purses her lips and makes wailing sounds, for example, and they laugh together. Or, if they're really angry with furrowed brows and deep voices, Holmes responds in the same way, saying: "Right, no smiling, no smiling." Often this kind of exaggerated response will nudge kids out of a bad mood.
—Used with permission from Jessica Holmes

Some families have established a Vision and Values Board that gives them a daily, visual reminder of where they want their family to be headed in the future and what beliefs or values will guide them on their journey. They celebrate their accomplishments in the belief that optimistic and resilient children are the result of optimistic parenting.

Other Laughter Organizations

The Association for Applied and Therapeutic Humor (AATH) is an international community of professionals who incorporate humour into their daily lives. AATH advertises itself as the leader in providing evidence-based information about current research and practical applications of humour. AATH disseminates information about humour and laughter through its conferences, publications and website. Its goal is to promote humour as a potential solution for any challenge one might face, from the everyday to the extreme.

You may also choose to investigate the **Laughter Yoga Institute**, founded by Jeffrey Briar and **The American School of Laughter Yoga**, led by Sebastien Gendry. These organizations are additional sources of training and information for those who want to learn more about laughter and share the message with others.

Twenty-One Laughter Benefits for Kids

Older children will find it informative to research each of the benefits of this rich, deep and relatively new field of therapeutic laughter. The twenty-one benefits are divided into three main areas:

Your body
Your mind
Your relationships

Laughter Makes Your Body Feel Better (physical)

1. Speeds up the heart and decreases blood pressure for more energy
2. Increases lung capacity and oxygen flow to the heart, lungs and brain
3. Boosts the immune system to prevent coughs, colds and infections and diseases
4. Helps to speed healing
5. Causes stomach muscles to tighten and then relax, like "inner jogging" for our abdominal organs
6. Unwinds negative stress levels
7. Relieves pain

"Three to five minutes of intense laughter can double the heart rate — the equivalent of three strenuous minutes on a rowing machine."
—Dr. William Fry

Laughter Lifts Your Spirits (mental and emotional health)

Endorphins are the body's natural pain relievers that make us feel happy. Serotonin is another hormone released in the body as a natural antidepressant. Laughing prevents "hardening of the attitudes."

8. Is a major coping mechanism that increases happiness and self-confidence
9. Releases endorphins, which relieve pain, into the bloodstream
10. Releases serotonin into the bloodstream to give us more strength in difficult times
11. Lifts our mood to help us relax
12. Relieves fear, anger and boredom
13. Relaxes muscles so that it's easier to get to sleep
14. Enhances learning and creativity by stimulating the right side of the brain

"Laughter is to life what shock absorbers are to cars. It won't take the potholes out of the road, but it sure makes the ride smoother."
—Barbara Johnson

Laughter Improves Your Relationships With People

15. Helps you get along with other people socially
16. Attracts new friendships
17. Leads to trust, teamwork and higher morale in groups
18. Adds to getting along and enjoying being with others

19. Creates stronger bonds and loving relationships between people
20. Contributes to the sense of belonging to a group
21. Is contagious and encourages more conversation and eye contact

These benefits last longer than the time spent laughing. Researchers say that the effects can be felt for twelve to twenty-four hours after the event. There are also other bonuses to laughter: it is one hundred percent transfat free, costs nothing, is the same in every culture and sounds the same in any language.

Laughter doesn't have to be heard to have an effect. Even looking forward to something that will be fun provides similar benefits.

Think of laughter as an adjunct to mainstream therapies such as art and music therapy. The rich body of gelotology research is growing every year, proving the undeniable benefits of therapeutic laughter. The old saying that "laughter is the best medicine" is based on more scientific proof than ever before. We have learned more about the benefits of laughter in the last ten years than in the previous one hundred. Simply put, if you want to live better, laugh more.

> *"Laughter is like a whole bunch of bubbles that tickle you from the inside."*
> —Winston, almost four years old

Activity — Blood Pressure Test

You will need the assistance of an adult to do this test. Use a blood-pressure cuff to test the physical benefit of lowering your blood pressure by laughing.

A) Take your blood pressure before you start this activity and record the reading.
B) Then, climb on the Laughter Ladder and try some different laughs. Think of a funny experience that happened to you, or get together with a friend who always makes you laugh.
C) Take your blood pressure reading after five to ten minutes of laughter. It should be lower than the initial reading.

Laughter Songs

The World Laughter Tour ANTHEM

"S-M-I-L-E": An American Melody

Sung To: "Battle Hymn of the Republic"

1st Verse

It isn't any trouble just to S-M-I-L-E
It isn't any trouble just to S-M-I-L-E
So smile when you're in trouble,
It will vanish like a bubble,
If you'll only take the trouble just to S-M-I-L-E.

Chorus:
Ha-Ha-Ha-Ha-Ha-Ha-Ha-Ha!
Hee-Hee-Hee-Hee-Hee-Hee-Hee-Hee!
Ho-Ho-Ho-Ho-Ho-Ho-Ho-Ho!
Ha-Ha-Hee-Hee-Ho-Hee-Ho!

(Repeat chorus after each verse.)

2nd Verse:

It isn't any trouble just to L-A-U-G-H
It isn't any trouble just to L-A-U-G-H
So laugh when you're in trouble,
It will vanish like a bubble,
If you'll only take the trouble just to L-A-U-G-H.
(Repeat chorus.)

3rd Verse:
It isn't any trouble just to G-R-I-N, grin
It isn't any trouble just to G-R-I-N, grin
So grin when you're in trouble,
It will vanish like a bubble,
If you'll only take the trouble just to G-R-I-N, grin.
(Repeat chorus.)
4th Verse:
It isn't any trouble just to Ha-Ha-Ha-Ha-Ha
It isn't any trouble just to Ha-Ha-Ha-Ha-Ha
So "HA" when you're in trouble,
It will vanish like a bubble,
If you'll only take the trouble just to Ha-Ha-Ha-Ha-Ha.
(Repeat chorus.)

Dem Laughing Bones

This is a variation on an old song.
Note the "funny bones" on the skeleton.

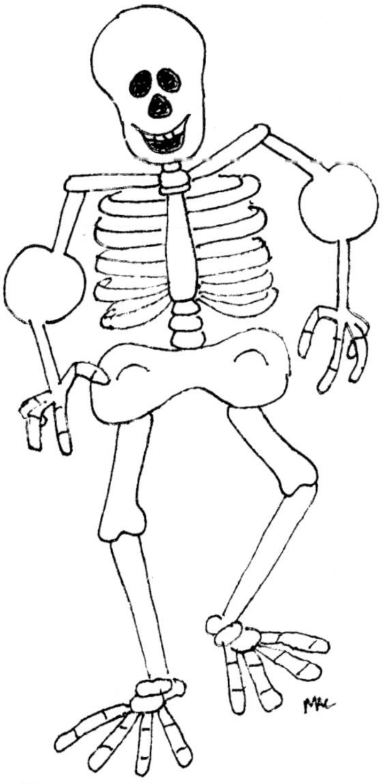

Dem bones, dem bones, dem funny bones,
Dem bones, dem bones, dem funny bones,
Dem bones, dem bones, dem funny bones,
Now shake dem laughing/ skeleton bones!

The toe bone's connected to the foot bone,
The foot bone's connected to the ankle bone,
The ankle bone's connected to the leg bone,
Now shake dem skeleton bones!

The leg bone's connected to the knee bone,
The knee bone's connected to the thigh bone,
The thigh bone's connected to the hip bone,
Now shake dem skeleton bones!

Dem bones, dem bones, dem dry bones,

Dem bones, dem bones, dem dry bones,
Dem bones, dem bones, dem dry bones,
Now shake dem skeleton bones!

The hip bone's connected to the back bone
The back bone's connected to the neck bone,
The neck bone's connected to the head bone,
Now shake dem skeleton bones!

The finger bone's connected to the hand bone,
The hand bone's connected to the funny bone,
The funny bones connected to the shoulder bone,
Now shake dem skeleton bones!

Dem bones, dem bones gonna walk around
Dem bones, dem bones, gonna walk around
Dem bones, dem bones, gonna walk around
Now shake dem skeleton bones!

—Adapted from the original song.
Original composer and copyright unknown.

Watch Dancing Bones on YouTube and then make your own video to these words. Remember to laugh a lot while singing it!

Question: Why was the skeleton studying anatomy?
Answer: He wanted to bone up on the subject.

Risibility

Somebody grinned and that started a smile.
Somebody chuckled and after a while,
All of us started to giggle with glee.
Everyone ended up howling with me.

Hee hee hee hee hee hee
Ho ho ho ho
Ha ha ha ha ha ha ha
Ho ho ho ho

Note: Risibility is the ability or tendency to laugh.
—from Anne Harmen, Retired Teachers of Ontario member at a Laughter Club, 2012

I Love to Laugh

Mary Poppins, a favourite old movie for many children, has a special song the characters all sing called "I Love to Laugh". If you can watch the movie or find it on YouTube, you'll see something special that happens when they sing this song!

Other Songs That Make You Smile

Start a list of the songs that make you smile and/or laugh.
Here's a sampling:

- Bobby McFerrin's "Don't Worry, Be Happy"
- Green Day's "It's Gonna Be a Good Day"
- Have a look on YouTube at the "A Tooty Ta Dance"
- The Monkey's "Good Vibrations"
- Three Dog Night's "Joy to the World"
- James Taylor's "You've Got a Friend"
- Roger's and Hammerstein's "Happy Talk", from the musical South Pacific

Activity Celebrate Funny Days of the Year

You can always find a reason to celebrate laughter every day. In addition to birthdays and holidays, add these to your calendar and get ready to celebrate:

- January 24—Global Belly Laugh Day
- February 11—Get A Different Name Day
- April—National Humour Month
- First Saturday of May—Free Comic Book Day (visit participating comic book stores across North America)
- First Sunday in May—World Laughter Day
- May 15—National Chocolate Chip Day
- June 14 - World Juggling Day
- First week in August—National Clown Week
- August 30—National Toasted Marshmallow Day
- September 19—Talk Like a Pirate Day
- October—first Friday - World Smile Day
- December 4—Cookie Day
- December 21—Look At the Bright Side Day

Note: Visit www.brownielocks.com for up-to-date, accurate, fun, serious and traditional holidays and theme days in the USA.

Activity Happiness Line and Laughter

As a way of remembering the lessons you have learned, pay this information and these activities forward and share ideas with other people you know. The best way to learn something is to do something with it!

Now that we have come to the end of Part Two: LOL—Laughing Out Loud, refer to the following Happiness Line and reflect on how the information and activities in this section affect your rating on the Happiness Line.

10 Extremely happy (feeling ecstatic, joyous, fantastic)

9 Very happy (feeling really good, elated)

8 Pretty happy (spirits high, feeling good)

7 Mildly happy (feeling fairly good and somewhat cheerful)

6 Slightly happy (just a bit above normal)

5 Neutral (not particularly happy or unhappy)

4 Slightly unhappy (just a bit below neutral)

3 Mildly unhappy (just a bit low)

2 Pretty unhappy (somewhat “blue”, spirits down)

1 Very unhappy (depressed, spirits very low)

0 Extremely unhappy (utterly depressed, completely down)

The Fordyce Emotions Survey. Michael Fordyce. *Social Indicators Research* 20,355-381. Jan. 28, 2006. Reprinted with permission from Springer Publishers.

We have completed our investigation of happiness and laughter. Now it’s time to complete the journey with a detailed examination of humour and comedy.

Implementation Ideas: LOL—Laughing Out Loud

Testing the Water

Observe spontaneous laughter in conversations with comments and stories.

Listen for the sounds at each step of the Laughter Ladder.

Watch for the power of a simple smile.

Be aware of the guidelines for safe laughter.

Getting Your Feet Wet

Start using the daily practices of Good-Hearted Living.

Try the laughter exercises with kids.

Play games that are fun with kids.

Experience the benefits of laughter—for your body, mind and relationships.

Learn how to sing the World Laughter Tour Anthem.

Observe how smiling and laughing can increase your range on the Happiness Scale.

Jumping in the Deep End

Become a Certified Laughter Leader with the World Laughter Tour.

Bring kids and seniors together in an intergenerational laughter club.

Become a member of AATH.

Teach the key messages to someone else and pay it forward.

Dig into the resources to learn more.

What implementation ideas would you add?

Resources on Laughter

Books

Briar, Jeffrey et al. (2011). *Laughter Revolutionaries : Making the World Safe for Hilarity*. CreateSpace.

Briar, Jeffrey. (2013 release date) *The Laughter Revolution: How Laughter Will Save the World.*

Farmer, Karen. (2007). *I Love to Laugh!: a book of fun and giggles.* Carlsbad. CA: Penton Overseas, Inc.

Franzini, Louis. (2001). *Kids Who Laugh: How to Develop Your Child's Sense of Humor.* Garden City Park, NY: Square One Publishers.

Kataria, Madan. (2012). *The Inner Spirit of Laughter: Five Secrets from the Laughing Guru.* available for download from www.laughteryoga.org.

Klein, Allen. (1998) *The Courage to Laugh: Humor, Hope and Healing in the Face of Death and Dying.* New York, NY: Penguin Putnam Inc.

Loomans, Diane and Kohlberg, Karen. (1993). *The Laughing Classroom: Everyone's Guide to Teaching with Humor and Play.* Novado, CA: New World Library.

Martin, Rod. (2007). *The Psychology of Humor: An Integrative Approach.* Burlington, MA: Elsevier Press.

McGhee, Paul. (2002). *Understanding and Promoting the Development of Children's Humor.* Dubuque, IA: Kendall Hunt Publishing.

O'Donnell, Rosie. (1997). *Kids Are Punny: Jokes Sent by Kids to the Rosie O'Donnell Show.* Warner Books
(and 30 minute HBO program on VHS, proceeds go to Rosie's For All Kids Foundation, devoted to children's charities)

Provine, Robert T. (2000). *Laughter: a Scientific Investigation.* New York: NY: Penguin Books.

Stephenson, Susan and Thibault, Paul. (2006). *Laughing Matters: Strategies for Building a Joyful Learning Community*. Bloomington, IN: Solution Tree Press.

Apps that are available for your electronic devices, such as:

Gratitude Stream—a "global" stream of good thoughts and thanks

iLaughOutLoud—contagious laughter

The LAUGHMAN—Doug Collins—most contagious laugh

Laugh Bag—nineteen laughs

Live Happy—positive psychology

Track Your Happiness

Websites

Allen Klein, Jollytologist—www.allenklein.com

American School of Laughter Yoga—www.laughteryogaamerica.com

Association for Applied and Therapeutic Humor—www.aath.org

Bernie DeKoven (games and more)—www.deepfun.com

Laughter Arts and Sciences Foundation—www.laughterfoundation.org

Laughter Yoga Institute—www.LYInstitute.org

School of Laughter Yoga—www.laughteryoga.org

World Laughter Tour—www.worldlaughtertour.com

World Smile Day—www.worldsmileyday.com

www.YouTube.com—search for JoyfulGent to see Jeffrey Briar's collection of short videos demonstrating various laughs

www.YouTube.com—search for World Laughter Tour clips

CDs, DVDs and Games

Good Morning Miss Toliver. PBS. (1993) 27 min. *Laughology*—available at www.laughology.info

The Laughter Video—available from Allen Klein. www.allenklein.com

Live at the London Paladium. Victor Borge, Danish pianist and comedian. (Punctuation routine.)

The Science of Laughter —DVD by Dr. Lee Berk

Don't Make Me Laugh game—for ages 12-200, LOLO Company

Part Three

Loosen Up Your Funny Bones

Question: Why are cats such bad dancers?
Answer: They have two left feet.

While Part One focused on the range of emotions and feelings associated with happiness, and Part Two dealt with laughter and its benefits, Part Three deals with recognizing, developing and sharing your sense of humour with others.

We all react to humour differently. For example, have you ever found a joke or a scene in a movie hilariously funny while a friend of yours had the opposite reaction? The resolutions you made in Your Happiness Project activity in Part One all took you on a search for happiness. How many of them would you call "funny"—how many of them made you smile or even laugh? You don't have to be smiling or laughing to be happy, but they often seem to go together.

Part Three explores these areas:

- How our individual senses of humour reflect different strengths, personalities and intelligences
- How various forms of humour and comedy can be playful and funny
- How humour can, unfortunately, be mean and hurtful.

So What Is a Funny Bone Anyway?

Children will be surprised to know that they have a funny bone, and that medically their funny bone is not a bone at all. Everybody has a "funny bone" in each elbow; it's really the ulnar nerve running just under the skin along the inside of the arms and connecting the feelings in the fourth and fifth fingers through the elbow to the brain. The medical term for the elbow bone is the humerus bone. Perhaps that's where the term "funny bone" comes from—it's the "humourous" bone.

When this nerve is tapped or hit, it bumps against the elbow bone and tingles in a funny or odd way. It may feel numb or frozen. Some people are more sensitive and say it hurts, but it doesn't do any lasting damage. This, of course, is where the expression that something "tickled the funny bone" comes from. It could be a joke or a funny face or a funny comic strip. In this sense, everyone's "funny bone" is uniquely his or her own.

Who's a fan of being tickled?

The other part of the saying "tickle my funny bone" is the word "tickle". Some children love being tickled. Ticklers can tickle someone (the ticklee) with their fingers to show affection. Most often the response is pleasurable and sometimes gets both people involved giggling and laughing—if they feel safe and trust each other. Some people are more ticklish than others. Some spots on the body are more ticklish and automatically make us laugh more - like armpits, feet, neck and under the chin. Even though laughter from tickling isn't associated directly with humour but more with our reflexes, it still makes us laugh.

Some people like to be tickled and some people truly hate it. Some people are afraid of being tickled and get embarrassed. Just as with any kind of touching and getting into people's personal space, the decision to tickle may be misinterpreted and/or unwanted. Ask kids what "tickle" means to them and if they like it.
Did you know that it's impossible to tickle yourself?

Tickle Me Elmo Doll
Many people are collectors of the famous Tickle Me Elmo Doll that first appeared in toy stores in 1996. The more you press Elmo in different places the more he rolls around, bends over and shakes – giggling all the while. He even says, "That tickles!" Even watching Elmo as he's being tickled contagiously spreads laughter throughout a group. As Robert Provine says, "There's a lot of science in Elmo."

The brain seems to be able to tell the difference between being tickled by someone else and trying to tickle yourself. Your brain cancels the tickle response. If this weren't the case, people might be "constantly tickling themselves accidentally".—Provine, 2004

A Playful Attitude

> *"We do not stop playing because we grow old, We grow old because we stop playing."*
> —Benjamin Franklin

While play, humour and sense of humour are all different, they are often seen as parts of the same process that leads to laughter. Let's look at what "play" is first, and then we can describe humour in more detail as a type of play. A sense of humour is the ability to amuse ourselves and others, and varies greatly between people. It may or may not result in laughing. I believe a sense of humour can be awakened and learned and is based on a playful attitude.

We use the word *play* to refer to activities such as board games or soccer or baseball, but play is far more complex than we might assume at first glance, and many researchers disagree on how to define it. A distillation of the many definitions boils down to this: At its core, play is an attitude or a spirit of fun and lightheartedness. It is *how* we do what we like to do in life. Play is the spontaneous expression of childlike qualities of inventiveness, curiosity and excitement. It can lead to doing silly stuff—and that's a good thing.

"When I'm having fun, I skate my best."
—Cindy Klassen

Cindy is the only Canadian Olympian to win 5 medals in a single Olympic games and the first female long track speed skater to win 5 medals in a single games at the 2006 Winter Olympics in Turin.

Louis Franzini cautions us in *Kids Who Laugh* (2012) that "play is simply what young children do. It is not particularly a way for them to have fun, as adults understand it, or to experience humour." (p. 37) They are simply playing—that's what kids do as they explore and grow. He goes on to say that, "fun experiences are something different from children demonstrating their sense of humour. Eventually, though, play does become associated with fun and with humour as we grow older."

Adults play too—when they find the time! A playful attitude or spirit is required to open the door to humour, a type of intellectual play, and to nurture our sense of humour to make others laugh and to laugh ourselves.

Play Can Be Serious and Fun

The words *play* and *work* don't seem to fit together in the same sentence, but they do have a common ground. Play has nothing to do with laziness. It is possible to love your work and to have fun while you are at work. Many companies and schools have an attitude that encourages lighthearted play with colleagues. Some workplaces believe that if the atmosphere is playful, people are more creative and get more work done in a shorter time. Solutions to very complex work problems emerge when people have some freedom, enthusiastic support and camaraderie at work. It can be the same in a classroom or during family times at home.

Play can be happy fun or it can be serious work. When individuals write the lyrics to a new song or redecorate a room or put together the menu for a fantastic meal, they are playing if they're having fun. It can look serious to someone watching them. They may not even be smiling. But, if they like it, it's fun!

- Can you be more creative when you are in a playful state of mind?
- How playful and fun is your classroom or your family time together?
- Can you think of a time when you were serious while you played? Can seriousness and play both work together in the same situation?

Note: SERIOUSLY! is a creative documentary created by Gwen Gordon about the power of play to generate and restore health and sanity to our world. www.seriouslythemovie.com

Eight Play Personalities

What one person does for fun may be a painful experience for someone else. For example, someone might have fun playing chess, while it would be torture for his or her friend. We each tend to have a dominant type of play personality. Often, several types can 'come into play' together. Stuart Brown, the founder and president of the nonprofit National Institute for Play, observed eight play personalities in his book *Play: How It Shapes the Brain, Opens the Imagination and Invigorates the Soul*:

"To love what you do, and know that it matters.
How could anything be more fun?"
—Katherine Graham

1. **The Joker**—the most basic and extreme player, makes people laugh, plays practical jokes and loves nonsense, could become "the class clown"

2. **The Kinesthete**—needs to move in order to think, loves all things involving movement, like dance, yoga, hiking, swimming
3. **The Explorer**—seeks out new experiences in play, physically, mentally and emotionally, likes going to new places and meeting new people
4. **The Competitor**—wants to win and be Number One in games or any form of competition, has fun keeping the score for everyone
5. **The Director**—loves being in charge and leading and organizing events and experiences like parties and camping trips
6. **The Collector**—finds enjoyment in finding, sorting through and collecting objects like comic books or experiences like going to concerts
7. **The Artist/Creator**—finds joy in creating or making things with his or her hands, for example in sculpting, woodworking, knitting, decorating, painting
8. **The Storyteller**—loves to create original stories in books, plays, music, or cartoons or to perform as an actor or musician or to enjoy the stories produced by others

—Reprinted with permission from the author, Stuart Brown.

It's interesting to watch children experiment with these personality types, find the ones they have the most fun with and also discover themselves in situations where they use nonpreferred types.

Humour Is Intellectual Play

"Humour is the ability to see three sides of one coin."
—Ned Rorem, composer

Laughter and humour start to develop in children when they start making observations about what makes them laugh and what they could do to make others laugh with their words or actions. Humour can also come from the enjoyment of just watching funny things happen. Humour is intellectual or mental play that happens when something is funny.

Most humour isn't planned—it's spontaneous and erupts out of nowhere. Watch for these unexpected, hilarious moments of play and laughter. They can come from small things in life like accidentally wearing your clothes inside out, or from more intentional forms of comedy such as joke telling, cartoons, stories or TV shows.

Funprints and Funny Bones

Just as no two people have the same fingerprints, we each have our very own, personal funprint or sense of humour, based on what makes us happy and seeing the nonserious side of life. A funprint may or may not lead to laughing out loud. The amusement found in something funny can bring about a quiet smile or a loud guffaw. A child with a good sense of humour can use that comedic intelligence to make others as well as him- or herself laugh.

Most people say that a good sense of humour (or a well-defined funprint) is an important factor in choosing friends. We express our personalities through our unique senses of humour. No two people have the same funprint; the same thing can be humourous or funny to one person and not funny to another. That's what makes humour so mystifying. By connecting our

> *"Psychological research has linked a keen sense of humour in children to a greater degree of intelligence, more extensive creative abilities, more flexible thought processes, higher self-esteem, better developed self-control and many other attractive personality traits."* —Louis Franzini

funny bones to our head bones, playfulness may be the most important component in determining and maintaining a sense of humour.

Is Humour a Strength of Yours?

Refer back to the Twenty-four Signature Strengths in Part One. Is being funny and making others laugh a strong part of your personality —how you act and behave with others? Were any of your resolutions in your Happiness Project (Part One) related to fun, humour or play? If you answered "yes" to either of these questions, you are revealing a strength that makes you feel good about yourself.

Humour and play are the most fun of all the strengths, according to Seligman. He advises adults to name and reward all displays of any of the strengths as they observe them in normal daily activities. This makes children more likely to repeat using that strength and more able to identify the various strengths in themselves and others. Each child will develop four or five signature strengths as he or she grows up and discovers more personal talents and interests.

Activity Children's Strength Survey

In addition to a survey for adult strengths and the online questionnaire described in Part One, Seligman has provided a Children's Strengths Survey in his book *Authentic Happiness.* He uses the following two questions referring to humour strengths, with the responses to be either *very much like me, like me, neutral, unlike me, very much unlike me*:

1. "Most kids would say I am really fun to be around."
2. "When one of my friends is feeling down, or I am unhappy, I do or say something funny to make the situation brighter."

—Seligman, 2002. p. 242

After students have responded to these two questions, ask them to go back through the online survey questions, select the ones that referred to humour and play, and talk about those responses one at a time. Was "humour and play" one of the top five strengths?

Activity: How Much Fun Are You to Be With?

Ask kids to think about these three questions and choose the one most like them.

1. Do I have a great sense of humour that makes me and those around me laugh a lot?
2. Did I use to have a sense of humour, but lately it seems to be blocked or missing for some reason?
3. Do I feel like I don't seem to have a sense of humour?

Lighten Up and Improve Your Sense of Humour

Children who choose #3 may need some help developing their sense of humour. They are not alone—many people share the same interest in finding ways that work for them to lighten up. Here are seven actions that will help kids become real "humourologists" who practise the art and science of healthy humour:

1. Begin a Funprint Diary to record observations and track changes in their personal sense of humour as they grow older.
2. Search out funny entertainment over entertainment that is depressing or stressful.
3. Tell funny stories about themselves or their family.
4. Collect and surround themselves with fun stuff.
5. Go places with fun people.
6. Try new things.

Activity: My Friends' Funprints

Make a list of three things you like to do to have fun and play (your own funprint).

Next, think about two of your best friends and their funprints. How is your funprint the same as or different from theirs?

Compare your funprint with those of students you don't really know well. A new friendship might develop when you realize you have more in common than you think.

Activity: Tickling My Family Funny Bone

Write a story about a funny family memory. Share this story with family members and see if they remember it the same way.

Interview one or two family members about funny stories from when they were kids. What were the first jokes they remember hearing? There may be some stories and jokes you can tell other people.

Sue Chisholm tells a story about her five-year-old grandson coming in one day and tattling about something minor that his older sister had done to him. Sue replied, "When did you start going to tattler's school? How are you doing there?" They both laughed and he got the point in a gentle way. This wise use of humour, instead of a scolding or serious reply, eases the tension and you will feel better too!

Activity: Exploring Our Funprints

The purpose of this activity is to explore the diversity in senses of humour in a group—our funprints. It will also help participants experience and understand the difference between humour and laughter. Humour is a form of intellectual play and laughter is physiological—in the body. Finding the humour in cartoon comedy is definitely thinking in a playful way.

1. Collect a wide variety of thirty to forty cartoons from newspapers or cartoon collections that you think may appeal to different funprints, enlarge them so they are easy to read and spread them out for the group to analyze either on the walls or on tables.
2. Each person in the group gets four sets of coloured dots—one for "funniest", one for "okay", one for "groaners", and one for "not funny at all".
3. Ask participants to vote with their dots as they go around and experience each cartoon.
4. Once everyone has voted, have the group members total the coloured dots and see which cartoon had the most of each colour. Discuss the qualities of each group. Have a look at the cartoons that were "not funny". Everyone should be able to see the diversity and how individualized humour is based on his or her funprints. What makes one person laugh may get no reaction from, or even offend, another.

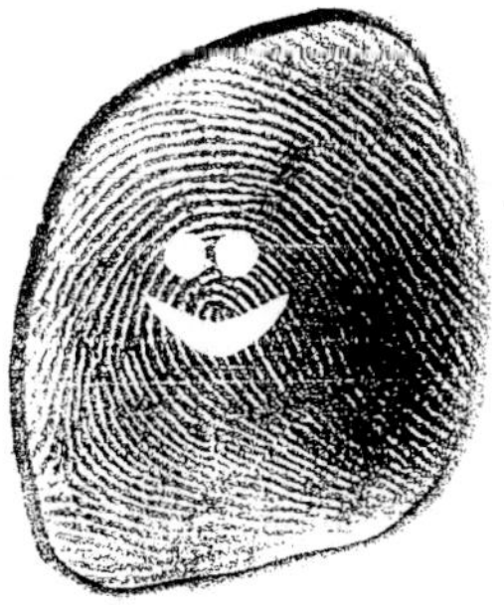

5. Someone who had a different opinion of a cartoon from the majority based on the dots may wish to explain why.
6. Extend the discussion by asking: Do we need some comedy stimulus to laugh or can we laugh without having something to laugh about? Can we laugh for no reason at all except for the pure joy that it brings?

—Included with permission from Lynne Hunter-Johnston, Certified Laughter Leader.

Activity My Funprint Movie

Developing a good funprint or sense of humour is one of the best things you can do for yourself at any age. It tickles your funny bone and makes you laugh. It can be there to help you lighten up when you are down. You can learn more about what makes other people laugh and how their funprints are different from yours!

Think about the questions that follow to get you started on your *Funprint Movie*. Then rehearse what you want to say in your script and choose where you want to film your movie using a video camera or a cell phone. Even a short three-to-five minute movie will be fun to make—and even more fun to show to others. Decide on a catchy title.

If you don't have the equipment to make a movie, try drawing a comic strip or writing a story about it instead. Here are some questions to get you started:

- How would I describe my funprint or sense of humour?
- How does it make me unique as an individual?
- What combination of Brown's Eight Play Personalities do I seem to have?
- How does my funprint make me and other people laugh?
- How ticklish am I? Do my family members like being tickled?
- Where did I get my funprint? Were there influences on me such as my parent(s), a relative, or maybe a favourite TV comedian?
- What's fun for me and makes me laugh - or even makes me smile inside? (For example, stand-up comedians, comic books, comedy films, cartoonists, TV sitcoms, or funny books.)
- How would someone who knows me well describe my funprint? (You could interview them to get some material for your movie.)

- Is there anything that hides my true funprint from others?
- What did I learn about myself from making this movie?

Stages of Humour Development

Most children start to look like they are smiling during their first month of life, but this "false smiling" is the result of internal changes and has nothing to do with humour at all. There are, however, stages of humour development in children beginning as early as two months.

Below is a summary of those stages. They are meant as general guidelines to help adults understand children's humour and what to expect as children grow intellectually, physically and emotionally. Humour specialist Paul McGhee says the age ranges represent the peak of humour associated with that stage. There is some predictability in the type of humour children prefer at specific ages, but there will always be individual differences. Try to watch for examples of each stage with your own children.

Birth to six months:
Laughter without any real humour
- Smiling starts at about two months as a form of communication
- Laughing out loud and giggling at almost anything for example, from tickling, or bouncing, and peek-a-boo games, music

Six to twelve to fifteen months:
Laughter at the attachment figure
- Laughing at someone's face like a parent's or something different and interesting—for example, silly faces, sounds or surprises, and physical play

Twelve to fifteen months to three to five years:
Treating an object as a different object
- Pretending for example—putting shoes up to their ear like a phone
- Beginning of the earliest kind of humour initiated by the child in make-believe play

Two to three or four years:
Misnaming objects or actions
- Hilariously using words that are wrong— for example, saying "lasterday" instead of yesterday
- Singing a new version of familiar songs— for example, "head, shoulders, knees & mommy"

Opposite—a special case of misnaming
- Giving the exact opposite of the correct word— for example, while playing Ring Around the Rosie, saying "Ashes, ashes we all fall up!"

Three to five years:
Playing with sounds (not meanings)
- Nonsense words emerge, sometimes repeating them—
- Reversing the tone of a funny book, from funny to serious
- Singing along with rhyming songs

Nonsense real-word combinations
- Using zany words—for example, "I want a peanut butter chair"
- Wearing funny props, hats

Distortion of features of objects, people or animals
- Adding or removing features that don't belong
- Changing the shape, size, colour, etc. of familiar things, drawin funny pictures

Gender reversal
- Having great fun using the opposite sex—for example, "Ha, Ha, Mary is a little boy"
- Wearing clothes and props from the other gender

Five to six or seven years:
Pre-riddle stage - transition period

- Multiple meanings start to be of interest
- Interested in verbal humour used by older kids
- Imitate what they hear others doing but don't make sense to adults—for example, "Knock-knock. Who's there? Nobody's home."

Seven to eleven years:
Riddles and jokes

- Understand riddles now and love using them
- Double meanings can be tricks
- Humour in the absence of actions begins.
- For the first time, they have the answer or witty comment that no one else has.
- Love exaggeration stories—for example, "It was so cold that". . . . , or "I went on the roller coaster so many times that. . ."
- Interested in gibberish and making up new languages
- Love performing any time, talent shows at home or school
- Love to read for fun

—Adapted from Paul McGhee, Permission Granted
See Dr. McGhee's website www.LaughterRemedy.com, for further details about these stages.

"The shift that occurs in children's humour at about age seven is more striking than at any other age....This is usually an exhilarating insight, and produces what some parents call riddle disease. . . .This makes the children capable for the first time of mentally moving back and forth between meanings and words—an essential skill for getting a punch line based on a pun. . . .This stage marks the first step into adult humour."
—Paul McGhee

Eleven to twelve years:
- Creating new humourous comments and funny situations
- Humour preferences start to emerge
- Aggressive and sexual content emerging

Thirteen and older:
- Much more adult-like in complexity
- Themes of irony and socially awkward situations
- Individual differences clearer now
- Beginning to be able to laugh at themselves
- Ridicule and insulting of others begins
- Time to deal with hurtful, unhealthy humour and discuss happier, healthy humour choices

—The final two stages, Louis Franzini, 2001.

Comedian Phyllis Diller said that becoming funny was her way of "adjusting to puberty. From twelve on, the only way to handle the terror of social situations was comedy—break the ice, make everybody laugh. I did it to make people feel more relaxed, including myself."

Parents and teachers need to be supportive of any child's attempts at humour from early childhood on. Families in particular influence a child's sense of humour. For example, children from families with challenges may develop a strong sense of humour in order to cope with what's going on at home. High-functioning families encourage children by their actions. Proudly letting our own sense of humour or funprint shine brightly with children will be key to giving them the permission to do the same—especially when we can laugh at ourselves.

Encourage kids who are naturally funny to use this unique intelligence in a positive way. You may find a budding comedian in your midst. Plan play breaks during the day with jokes and riddles. Devise a hand signal or routine to pull kids back.

Humour and Intelligence

Harvard Professor Howard Gardner is widely known for his *Theory of Multiple Intelligences*. He defines intelligence as the ability to solve a problem or create a product that is valued in a society. He has strict criteria for the identification of an intelligence, and so far, eight have been established. He says we all have one or two preferences that lead us to our best learning modes. From the following list, which ones do your children use the most? Which ones do they use to learn? Are there strong connections between their intelligences and their signature strengths?

Eight Types of Intelligence

- **Linguistic—**well-developed verbal skills and sensitivity to the sounds, meaning and play of words; talent for learning new languages, speaking in front of others
- **Logical-mathematical**—the ability to think abstractly, to use logical reasoning and recognize sequences, patterns and order with numbers
- **Musical**—sensitivity to pitch, rhythm and tone in music and beats
- **Visual-spatial**—the ability to think artistically in images and pictures
- **Bodily-kinesthetic**—the ability to use the body skillfully and handle objects skillfully
- **Interpersonal**—the ability to understand people's moods and relationships
- **Intrapersonal**—heightened awareness of another's feelings and who they are as a person; access to one's emotional life as a means to understand oneself and others
- **Naturalist**—the ability to connect with and understand the environment, weather, and plants

It takes different kinds of intelligence to have a good sense of humour and make ourselves and other people laugh. It turns out that the ability to appreciate and create humour and comedy involves a combination of intelligences.

We use logical intelligence to create amusing situations. We also use the personal intelligences (using the prefix *inter*, when amusing others and *intra*, when amusing oneself). Linguistic intelligence makes it easier for you to mix comedy into day-to-day conversations as well as tell and create jokes and other verbal forms of humour. We can compose funny songs or jingles with musical intelligence. Comedians draw upon interpersonal, linguistic and bodily-kinesthetic intelligences simultaneously. So, you can be smart and funny at the same time.

Enjoy the sense of humour that erupts from kids as they play by themselves or with others. Watch their excitement as you laugh along with the jokes and verbal humour they share with you. Look for humour around you as well. Kids will take your lead and follow the joking comments you make.

Note: Refer to the Additional Resources List for two of Howard Gardner's key books. To learn more about how a school has built on all of the intelligences, research the writings of Tom Hoerr, Head of School at New City School, St. Louis, Missouri. The faculty there has written extensively about how MI (Multiple Intelligences) can help students.

Making People Laugh

Humour has become a collective term for all things that make us laugh. It has been defined as a type of intellectual play that triggers laughter or amusement. On many occasions, humour and the laughter it unleashes are spontaneous, random events that come out of conversations or events, for example, watching someone accidentally squish open a juice box in his or her face.

On the other hand, **Comedy** is a more complicated form of planned humour deliberately created to make people laugh and to provide entertainment. The end result of active comedy may look easy, but it actually takes a clever concept, a careful set-up and good timing to create comedy in such things as TV shows or stand-up comedy routines. Some comedians make it a full-time job and earn a living from it.

Have you ever been hurt by someone who thought he or she was being funny? Comedy and humour can be far from funny if they are used to ridicule or embarrass others. You'll find out more about the mean, hurtful side of humour later in this book.

Personal Interactions with Humour

Children and adults can vary greatly in their interactions with humour. Individual differences for both groups can be measured by looking at the following factors:

- The ability to comprehend the humour: Do I get the joke?
- The ability to appreciate humour: Do I think that the joke is funny?
- The expression of humour: How do I show my enjoyment of humour?
- The active search for sources of humour: How much do I seek it out?

- One's memory for humourous events: Can I recall them enough to recount them?

All of the aspects of humour listed above are about being on the receiving end of humour. Those who create and/or produce comedy from humour, either spontaneously or on purpose, are special.

—Adapted from *The Psychology of Humor*. Rod Martin, 2007. p. 194

Unintentional Humour—or Maybe Not?

Sometimes something—an event or utterance—that wasn't meant to be funny is. For example, a man about to make an important and serious speech leans on a podium that then collapses. These types of "accidents" could truly be unintentional but are often used intentionally by comedy writers who know their effect.

Spend some time on the website www.fun-with-words.com to play with this form of humour. Older children could also research the origin of the following forms of unintentional humour.

Freudian slips are made when one word substituted for another seems to reveal something you're hiding or not really wanting to talk about. For example, "When you say one thing and mean your mother."

Malapropisms involve the misunderstanding and incorrect use of similar sounding words. Here are some examples:

- Worst-case *ontario.* (worst-case scenario)
- I'm not a pessimist, I'm an *optometrist.* (optimists and pessimists)
- He had to use a fire *distinguisher.* (extinguisher)
- Dad says the monster is just a *pigment* (figment) of my imagination.

- My sister has *extra-century* (extrasensory) perception.

Spoonerisms are phrases, sentences, or whole words where the initial sounds get switched. They are named after W.A. Spooner, an English clergyman known for this type of slip. Here are a few examples:

- "Tickle my funny bone" becomes "Fickle my bunny tone"
- "Laugh your head off" comes out as "Haugh your lead off"
- "My lips are zipped" becomes "My zips are lipped."
- "Go and take a shower" becomes "Go and shake a tower"
- "Sleepy time" becomes "teepy slime"

They are the funniest when the "spoonerized" words end up making sense and also being funny in the mixup. Creating these intentionally is a lot of fun.

Whole stories can be spoonerized. For some "tairy fales" visit the website www.matthewgoldman.com where you'll find new versions of stories such as *Rindercella*, *Pee Little Thrigs* and *Little Ride Hooding Red.*

Billboards and signs
Sometimes the comedy is right there in front of you if you just look around. Billboards and signs that people create on purpose or by accident are often hilarious in their final result.

Notes to teachers from parents

Parents write the funniest things to teachers in excuse notes for their children's absences from school. Here's a sampling:

- "Dear School: Please excuse John being absent on Jan. 28, 29, 30, 31, 32, and also 33."
- "Please excuse Gloria from Jim today. She is administrating."
- "Carlos was absent yesterday because he was playing football. He was hurt in the growing part."
- "My daughter is wearing a bra to school for the first time. Please make sure she doesn't take it off."
- "Please excuse Jennifer for missing school yesterday. We forgot to get the Sunday paper off the porch, and when we found it Monday, we thought it was Sunday."
- "Please excuse Jason for being absent yesterday. He had a cold and could not breed well."

Howlers from kids on tests

Teachers never look forward to hours of marking tests and assignments, even though they know it's part of the reality of assessment. The occasional funny comment from a student can make the task easier. Teachers often keep scrapbooks or journals full of these so they can look back at them later. They make a great conversation starter between parents and teachers.

Here are some examples from an English teacher's journal after a lesson about metaphors and analogies:

- Her face was a perfect oval, like a circle that had its two sides gently compressed by a Thigh Master.
- She had a deep throaty laugh just like a dog before it throws up.
- The little boat gently drifted across the pond exactly the way a bowling ball wouldn't.
- Her hair glistened in the rain like nose hair after a sneeze.
- His thoughts tumbled in his head, making and breaking alliances like underpants in a dryer without Cling Free.

Robert Nielsen, a veteran English teacher and author, compiled these examples in a book he edited titled *Breeding as a Sport: 101 Student Howlers,* as he conscientiously graded his exam papers searching for the "possibility of encountering a howler" along the way. Here are a few of his best finds:

- Textbooks are all right but if you want somebody to learn something put it inside a television and watch them grasp it.

- Question: Who was Magellan? Answer: The man who circumcised the world.
- Question: Give the degrees of bad. Answer: Bad, worse, dead.
- So often, sentences are not really sentences. It is important to make sure each sentence expresses a complete
- Relative humidity—That is why children look like their parents.
- Benjamin Franklin invented bifocals so he could always see both sides of the question.
- Question: What does "lighthearted" mean? Answer: It means when you're not married.

—Reprinted with permission from Robert Nielsen

Funny letters kids write to parents

Of course, parents are the recipients of some very cute and incredibly funny notes. Here are three from a *Kids Write The Darndest Things: The Funniest Letters From Children,* published on www.huffingtonpost.com.

Dear Camron
I am so sory that I smaced you in the privets.

Dear Mom,
Day 5 of camp is a lot better. The rash on my P-nus is gone and now I can run. My friends hate when I say eggs so I'm trying to stop saying it.
Love, Josh

Mom,
I'm going to run away tomroe at 9:30 wean you and Dad are steeping. Be sure to say goodby forever. Emily
P.S. I will be packnd tonight

Teacher/principal bloopers

Of course, teachers and principals also say goofy things and make funny bloopers from time to time. Be on the lookout for any of these and keep track of them—we need to balance the blame. Here are two announcements that were heard over the P.A. system:

All students P through U go to the auditorium now.

All those boys with blown up balls report to the principal's office.

Creating Comedy: Written and Performed

Much of the attention in the research on comedy has been focused on verbal jokes and cartoons (visual jokes), but there is a much larger world of comedy to explore! Whether kids of any age (even the child deep inside all adults) want to create their own comedy or simply want to appreciate comedy, there are many forms with which to experiment. When children start to explore, they will find it challenging to sort out the many subtypes that seem to cross over each other. As we explore a few of them, you will get ideas for both appreciating them as well as tips for creating comedy. Children should be exposed to as many forms of humour as possible, keeping in mind their age and maturity level. They may even catch on to a type of comedy that could lead to a hobby or even a career.

A useful method of sorting the creators of comedy that children can understand centres around two main categories:

a) Writers of comedy
b) Performers of comedy

The writers category includes people who prefer to create comedy behind the scenes for others to experience or perform. Here are some examples:

- Script writers for comedy movies, TV, situational comedies (sitcoms) and ads on TV or the Internet
- Authors of funny stories, books, plays and poetry
- Lyricists of humourous songs and jingles
- Cartoonists for newspapers, comic strips, animation and comic books (using a visual form of communicating written words and ideas)

It is estimated that situational comedy is the single largest slice of the television industry outside of news and current affairs.

The performance category includes people who like to be out there in front of other people delivering comedy in a visual or verbal way. Performance comedy can be either spontaneous or scripted. Here are some examples:

- Stand-up comedians, comedic actors
- Clowns, including therapeutic clowns
- Improvisational artists
- Singers and musicians

Some comedians do both the writing and performing; for example, a stand-up comedian may write his or her own jokes. There are many possible combinations of written and performed comedy—they are not necessarily independent of each other.

The following pages will help you:

- Clarify the unique features of each type of comedy
- Provide strategies for kids to try out each type

A) Writers of Comedy

In this section, you will learn about three of the many forms of laughs that comedic writers use as they play with words: puns, jokes and riddles. Children love all of them once they reach the age of six or seven years old and have the vocabulary to understand them. Writers with a playful attitude take everyday situations and human predicaments and exaggerate them into the realm of the ridiculous. They put items or ideas together that seem to be incompatible and build up to surprise endings for their punch lines.

"Comedy is two opposite ideas that collide." —Charlie Chaplin

1. **Puns**

A pun is a sentence in which one set of words produces two different meanings. Riddles and many jokes are based on humourous puns. Parents and teachers often groan when they hear a pun which makes kids laugh even harder. If you tell one and they groan at you—it's a winner! To get the hang of them you will need to focus on multiple meanings of words or interpretations of the same event.

There are two main linguistic methods for creating puns:

- Homographic, in which the pun is based on a word with multiple meanings but the same spelling and same pronunciation. For example: "What do a tree, an elephant and a car all have in common? They all have trunks." or "I wondered why the baseball was getting bigger. Then it hit me." or "A bicycle can't stand alone. It is two tired."

- Homophonic, where the pun exploits two words with similar sounds with different spellings but similar pronunciation. For example: "A chicken crossing the road is pure poultry [poetry] in motion." or "Camping is intense." [in tents] or "There was a person who sent ten different puns to his friends, with the hope that at least one of the puns would make them smile. No pun in ten did."[intended] or "Police were called to a day care where a three-year old was resisting a rest." [resisting arrest]

The compound pun is one in which multiple puns are used for an additional effect. An example of this is the following story:

Two friends sitting in a kayak were chilly, so they lit a fire in the craft. Unsurprisingly, it sank, proving once again that you can't have your kayak and heat it too.

Here is a second compound pun.
Mahatma Gandhi walked barefoot most of the time, which produced an impressive set of calluses on his feet. He also ate very little, which made him rather frail, and with his odd diet he suffered from bad breath. This made him: A super calloused fragile mystic hexed by halitosis. [Supercalifragilisticexpialidocious] (from the Disney musical "Mary Poppins".)

Numerous other punster formats exist such as:

• Tom Swifties

These puns are named after a character in a comic strip called Tom Swift. He always ended his sentences with a punny adverb describing how he did it. (These examples were retrieved from the website for the magazine of the Boy Scouts of America www.boyslife.org.)

"Pass me the shellfish," Tom said crabbily.
"Help, my pants are falling off," Tom belted out.
"Boy this hotdog is delicious," Tom said frankly.

• Spoonerisms—see page 115

• Basic Knock, Knock jokes

I was sitting in a hospital waiting room one afternoon and watched a girl about five years old start telling her grandmother a long series of Knock, Knock jokes. She was delighted by each and every one of them, and her grandmother never gave up answering each one. After about ten minutes she had everyone in the waiting room laughing out loud—or at least smiling. It lightened the mood in a place that is usually so serious.

Knock, Knock.
Who's there?
Orange.
Orange Who?
Orange you glad I'm here!

Knock, Knock.
Who's there?
Denise.
Denise who?
Denise and de nephew are at the door.

Knock, Knock.
Who's there?
Turnip.
Turnip who?
Turnip the heat. It's freezing in here.

Knock, Knock.
Who's there?
Señor.
Señor who?
Señor underpants when you bent over.

• Daffynitions
These daffy redefinitions of words are fun to make up with a dictionary close by. Here are a few examples:

Microchips: Those crumbs at the bottom of the potato chip bag
Coffee: Someone who is coughed upon
Boomerang: What you say to frighten a meringue
Mushroom: A closet full of baby food
Addicted: When you can't stop doing math

Note: A pun differs from a malapropism in that a malapropism uses an incorrect expression that refers to another (usually correct) expression, but a pun uses a correct expression that refers to another (sometimes correct but more often absurdly humourous) expression.

Puns are often used in the punch line of a joke. So, practise making up your own punch lines to different jokes with puns of your own!

2. Riddles

Riddles are based on puns and involve a puzzling question with a double meaning that can be answered only with a funny (or punny) answer. It can be tricky when kids are writing riddles. The fun part is that only the child has the answer or punch line!

My teenaged granddaughter Katie and I were talking about riddles and trying to figure out a few this summer. She had been reading a Stephen King book called *The Waste Lands* in which the characters are challenged with a riddle from *Riddle-De-Dum!*, a book from which the answers have been ripped out. She told me it drove her crazy trying to figure it out as she repeated it in her head about eight hundred times! This riddle goes like this:

There is something that nothing is and yet it has a name.
It's sometimes tall and sometimes short, joins our talks, joins our sports, and plays in every game. What is it?

Although this example has nothing to do with humour, I was impressed with how she remembered the riddle and how it got her and her friends thinking about the answer as part of solving the story.

I don't want to spoil the suspense in case you haven't read the book. I will follow a method introduced by Paul McGhee of giving three clues to the solution to help you figure out the answer—if you haven't solved it already. See the following clues:

Clue 1: It rhymes with meadow.
Clue 2: It occupies all of the space behind an opaque object with light in front of it.
Clue 3: Look carefully at the boy with the guitar.

Here are some funny riddles:

How do you keep a fish from smelling?
Answer: Cut off its nose!

What did one eye say to the other eye?
Answer: Just between you and me, something smells.

Paul McGhee's book *Stumble Bees and Pelephones* helps kids create punch lines to riddles based on puns to improve their verbal humour skills. Eventually they start "thinking like a comedian" and can make up their own riddles. He has collected 250 riddles and jokes (easier, difficult and very difficult) with the punch line missing. Three clues are given to get the kids going and they have to use the information to create their own funny punch line. They read one clue at a time, covering the other clues with their hands. Kids can keep score and make it a game by the number of clues they need to solve the riddle. The answers are at the end of the book—if kids need them.

Here's an example from his book:
How do skunks say grace before their meals? "Let us ________."
1st clue: What do many families do just before they eat?
2nd clue: Another word for a fine mist.
3rd clue: You can paint things using this fine mist.

[The answer is "spray", silly.]

3. Jokes

You can have fun and be funny without telling any jokes, but good jokes are certainly very popular with kids young and old. Jokes are stories that are so funny that when you tell one, it makes people laugh and they're happy. Jokes also make you think. Jokes cover a wide territory in addition to puns and riddles.

Some kids start out their comedy career by performing jokes and funny stories they have heard, liked and memorized. While this is a good place to start, it's easier to just look around for funny ideas and play with words to write stories from life experiences. They won't forget the punch line and it's even funnier because it really happened!

Here are some sources of inspiration:
- A movie you just saw
- What your neighbour did lately that made you laugh
- Something your brother did on his first date
- A time when everyone just started laughing and you couldn't see why
- Something you did that was funny—laughing at yourself is a good way to start

Kids could start a blog as an online diary to practise their comedic writing, especially if they don't want to perform in public.

- Nonsense real-world combinations—use your imagination to change, twist or bend real-world things. Make animals do human things, like a cat playing the piano. Or, make humans do animal things like bark for attention.

- Change the words to nonsense words using gibberish. For example, the famous I Taut I Taw a Putty Tat (from the old *Tweety and Sylvester* TV cartoons).

- Think of something that happens and something that usually doesn't happen and put them both together. For example, Why did the chicken brush its teeth? Answer: To clean its eggs.

- 'What If' Stories—play make believe with 'what if' jokes. Here are some starters:

  What if we were born old and died young?
  What if teachers were the students and the students were the teachers?
  What if parents had no worries in the world?
  What if boys could do anything girls could do?
  What if we couldn't use humour anymore?

- Exaggeration—here are some starters:

  It was so cold today that. . . .

The field trip was so much fun we. . . .
I ate so much food that. . . .
She was so tall that. . . .

Adults may want to extend their child's repertoire by further examining these additional comedic writing themes:

- Oxymorons—mutually contradictory ideas like "jumbo shrimp" or "play school" or "artificial intelligence is no match for natural stupidity". George Carlin is famous for his observational skills with oxymorons.
- Goofy words in the dictionary such as: dinosaur names (Saltasaurus, Diplodocus, Utrasaurus), dog breeds (Yorkipoo, Goldendoodle, Shih Tzu), and wacky sounding words (tootsy, festoonery, kiskadee).
- Limericks—funny short poems with five rhyming lines and a very specific rhythm. (see www.gigglepoetry.com) Here's an example:

  There was a gourmet named Billy
  Who dined from Beijing to Chile
  His only complaint
  About the places he ate
  Was that chili in Chile was chilly
- Self-deprecating stories—putting yourself down, making fun of yourself by focusing on a mistake or a weakness.

Cartoons and Comics

Cartoons and comics have all the elements of regular comedic story writing; the difference is that the writers use drawings as well as the written word to communicate their messages to readers, often in sequential frames or panels. The writing may be in the form of captions or thought/speech bubbles. Most cartoons are hand-drawn, but computer-drawn cartooning is gaining in popularity. Many aspiring cartoonists begin by doodling shapes and characters on paper and refine their artistic skills in visual graphic arts courses at school or in the community.

Explore these types of cartoons:

- **Syndicated newspaper comic strips.** Some classic cartoon series include *Peanuts* by Charles M. Schultz, *Calvin and Hobbes* by Bill Waterson (about an adventurous little boy called Calvin with his imaginary pet tiger called Hobbes) and *Dennis the Menace* by Hank Ketcham. Kids today enjoy following strips such as *Zits*, *For Better or Worse*, and *Family Circus.*
- **Comic books.** In the 1950s, many artists drew cartoons for American Marvel and DC Comics with characters such as Superman, Batgirl and Wonder Woman, and magazines like *Mad.*
- **Caricatures.** A **caricature** is a portrait that exaggerates or distorts the essence of a person to create an easily identifiable visual likeness. (See the back of the book for caricatures of Sue and Tony.)
- **Editorial/political cartoons in magazines and newspapers.** These are particularly good for teaching pop culture issues, especially at election times.
- **Animation for TV or movies.** Movie studios like Disney make animated cartoons and movies that are favourites of children.
- **Anime.** Originating in Japan, this form of animation is found on TV, video, films or online. It can be hand-drawn or computer-animated and features colourful graphics and often adult themes.
- **Manga**. These comics are created by Japanese writers for males and females of all ages usually in paperback or graphic novel form. (See also webmanga.) Note: sometimes the same story is produced in both manga and anime.
- **Graphic novels.** This form of comedy involves a longer narrative and is most often in bound form. (The Canadian cartoonist Seth, the 2011 recipient of the Harbourfront Festival Prize and the first cartoonist to win, was acknowledged for having, "substantially contributed to the state of literature and books in Canada.")

"You start on a page with a quickly-thought-up idea and then just start going and I think that's the kind of stuff that comes right out of the information that floats around at the front of your brain."
—Seth, as quoted in "Graphic Work is Gaining Fans", *Toronto Star*, Oct. 21, 2011

All cartoonists need to learn how to develop an idea, lay out a page, use panels in different ways and draw characters in their own style.

Activity Your Favourite Cartoonists

Check out the Puzzles and Comics section in the weekend edition of your newspaper or look for cartoon books and movies in the library or bookstore.

Here are some to have a chuckle with:

- *Zits* by Jerry Scott and Jim Borgman
- *Mutts* by Patrick McDonnell
- *Sherman's Lagoon* by Jim Toomey
- *The Pajama Diaries* by Terri Libenson

"The best comics expose human nature and help us laugh at our own stupidity and hypocrisy. They indulge in exaggeration and absurdity, helping us see the world with fresh eyes and reminding us how important it is to play and be silly." —Bill Waterson, *The Calvin and Hobbes Tenth Anniversary Book.*

Activity... Could you be a Cartoonist?

Here is some advice from this book's illustrator, Tony MacKinnon—aka MAC. "Drawing cartoons is a lot of fun. It can be very relaxing and lets you communicate your thoughts and ideas in a very simple way. It is often said that "a picture is worth a thousand words" and with cartoons it's no different. Cartoonists can use an unlimited pool of methods and styles to highlight or describe any situation. Their own imagination is the limit. Like any other activity, whether for pleasure or work, practice makes perfect. Some of the best cartoonists are accomplished artists who have studied and practised their art for many years. Enjoying what you do makes the rest easy."

Starting points for cartooning:

- Go back to the jokes pages, and using the same ideas, draw the joke instead.
- Explore issues that are of personal interest to you.
- Try writing your own captions to cartoons.
- Draw a comic strip with your family as the characters in a new situation or wearing weird clothes.
- Draw your own greeting cards with cartoons for birthdays or special days to develop your style. Write funny messages for the cover and the inside page.

MAC says, "A very simple way to do many different characters is to add hats or head coverings to a circle. Using the same basic shape, you can create a huge number of familiar common people for any situation (sports, work, play, etc.). Add a nose, a bit of hair, colour, and you're in business." See the following page.

—Steps to draw characters from MAC.

Students can use their imaginations, develop their writing skills and have fun at the same time by creating their own comics and story lines. This is especially fun for kids whose first language is not English or for children with special needs.

Try these websites for web-based cartooning:
- www.pixton.com
- www.makebeliefscomix.com created by Bill Zimmerman

On YouTube, search for City College, N.Y. and teacher Tamara Kirson, named Teacher of the Year by the New York Times, for her positive experiences with Zimmerman's site and her English for Speakers of Other Languages (ESOL) students.

Available on this site is How to Play: For Educators—21 Ways to Use Makebeliefscomix.com in the Classroom to practise new vocabulary and conversational skills.

Following are three other websites to explore.

- www.marvelkids.marvel.com/games/play/75/create_your_own_comic Create your own comic strip or comic book using Marvel characters like Thor, Hulk, and Spider-Man
- www.stripgenerator.com
- www. plasq.com/products/comiclife2/mac

The cartoons that follow show different ways of making people laugh:

a)Putting two things together that don't belong together—like a cat playing a piano or a human with a dog's head.

b)Making things bigger or smaller—like a policeman with a tiny car.

Activity: Start with a Character

Use one or more of these characters for inspiration and include them in a one-panel comic or a multipanel comic strip. Or include yourself as a cartoon character.

Funny Literacy Activities: Using Humour to Help Kids Enjoy Reading

> *"Almost all children love funny books, it's what helps hook them into the reading habit."* —Michael Rosen, U.K. Children's Laureate

You will definitely want to visit www.humormonth.com to read more about the *Funny Certified Laughter Reader Literacy Project* activities. National Humor Month, which kicks off each year on April Fool's Day (of course), was founded by Larry Wilde, Director of the Carmel Institute of Humor. Steve Wilson, Joyologist and Founder of *World Laughter Tour*, is the Director of National Humor Month since 2008.

At the website www.humormonth.com, you can read about the *Funny Certified Laughter Reader Literacy Project.* Its purpose is to encourage children to read funny books, graphic novels, comic books and stories, alone or with their classmates or families, with the incentive of becoming a Certified Laughter Reader. Humourous literature is often overlooked as a valuable way to increase the love of reading.

Kids who complete a prescribed reading activity during April (for example, one hour per week of funny books, in fifteen minute intervals) plus a follow-up activity (for example, tell a joke, write a poem, create a comic strip or draw a funny picture), will receive the designation of Certified Laughter Reader. There is a sample reporting form and certificate on the site.

The website offers a sample list of funny picture books, easy readers (such as the *Amelia Bedelia* series by Peggy Parish), juvenile fiction, jokes and riddles, and goofy poetry. Consult with your school librarian or public library for more suggestions.

If you would like to participate or start a pilot project, call or e-mail Steve Wilson to register at www.worldlaughtertour.com or www.humormonth.com or phone 1-800-NOW-LAFF (669 -5233).

Note: A website to visit is www.lazyreaders.com—the brainchild of Danny Brassel, another man who loves reading. This is a book club with recommendations of books for all ages that are fun to read for personal enjoyment.

Dav Pilkey is best known as the author and illustrator of the *Captain Underpants* book series, much loved by children. Dav did a book-signing in my hometown of Brampton recently. I stood in line with hundreds of excited kids and their parents to get Dav's autograph and a photo with him on a Friday after school at a Chapter's Bookstore. Many of the kids were dressed as

Captain Underpants with their white underwear proudly worn on top of their clothes (where else?) and a red cape. The kids I had a chance to talk with were well versed in the adventures of all of the characters in the series—now in the ninth epic novel. One father told me that his son didn't like reading until they found Dav Pilkey. One day, his son was asked to come to school dressed as a literary figure—and he went dressed as Captain Underpants.

Doing some research on Dav's website www.pilkey.com will give you a unique window into his world as a young boy and student when his intelligence and skill weren't appreciated at all. Here is an excerpt:

After setting the school's all-time record for the amount of time spent in the principal's office, Dav was diagnosed with Attention Deficit Disorder and severe hyperactivity. By the start of first grade, Dav had successfully moved into the role of class clown. He was the undisputed king of funny noises, and held the classroom record for the number of crayons he could stick up his nose at one time (a record he holds to this day).

Everybody in Dav's class thought he was pretty funny, except for one person—his teacher! Dav's teacher didn't care for his particular brand of humor, so she began sending him out into the hallway. Before long, Dav was spending so much time in the hall that his teacher moved a little desk out there for him.

B) Performers of Comedy

> *"The whole object of comedy is to be yourself, and the closer you get to that, the funnier you will be."*—Jerry Seinfeld, comedian

While it involves risk to get up in front of people with the intention of making them laugh, it can bring out the inner clown in all of us. Comedic performers use their faces and bodies to add physicality and emotion to humour. It can be anything from total free-for-all ad libbing (making comedy up in the moment), to a loose script outline that is improved as it is performed, to a tightly scripted comedy routine.

Charlie Chaplin, one of the most famous mimes (see page 156), used this technique because his movies were silent. Marcel Marceau, pictured here, was an internationally acclaimed French actor and mime most famous for his persona as Bip the Clown. (You can check him out on YouTube) Today, street theatre and buskers carry on the tradition of mime using little or no dialogue and lots of body movement and expression.

Following are three types of comedic performers you can talk to children about. Mime can be a part of all three of these.

a) improvisation (improv) artists
b) clowns—theatrical, therapeutic and circus clowns
c) stand-up comedians

Note: See page 156 for a list of the forms of comedy.

The book *Made You Laugh* by Joel Garner (2004), with its treasure-filled DVD of actual footage, is an excellent reference book for a detailed history of comedy in radio, television, stand-up and movies. It is highly recommended to supplement this material.

Improv Artists

*My thanks go to Gord McGiverin, teacher, improv coach and performer, for the generous contribution of this section on improv.

Improv is a great way to perform comedy and have fun with kids, be they seven or seventy years old. Because improv is all about making things up on the spot, anyone can play—and you don't need any 'stuff' to do it. All you need is a willingness to play and to explore ideas that are offered to you.

Rapping and hip hop are examples of improv performance styles. In fact, most of our behaviour in life is improv, reacting in the present moment. Improv is simply the spontaneous creation of a scene or scenes involving one or more people being somewhere, doing something.

For example, you might be given the following suggestion for a scene:

This scene takes place in a pet store and is between a customer and a salesperson.

That is all the information that's needed to create an improvisation.

One of the great things about improv is that it is so adaptable. You could do the above scene with just one couple performing the scene or by having a large group, divided into pairs, all doing that scene at the same time. Simply count them down "5—4—3—2—1—Begin." You can give them a one-minute warning once they've gotten into the scene, so they can try to find an ending at more or less the same time. (That is for your benefit, not theirs) Of course, a large room where kids can spread out is a big help. If one is not available, simply have half the group go at a time, while the others watch. Then reverse, and let the other half do their scenes. This is a good approach to begin with, especially for absolute beginners, because the threat of performing in front of a group is minimal when everyone goes at once. Of course, the makeup of the group, the confidence level, and the physical space you are working in will be deciding factors in how to begin. Once the kids are comfortable, have them present their scenes with just their partners. Keep the scenes on the short side and have them change partners regularly so they get used to working with everyone, not just their close friends.

Obviously, the focus at the outset is to ensure that kids become familiar with the process of improv and have fun while doing so. The pressure to "perform" should not be a big factor. Another of the joys of teaching improv is that there is no right or wrong. Because everything that is said is made up on the spot, and since you cannot predict what another person is going to say, you can only choose how to respond. Naturally, some choices make more sense or are easier to work with than others, but there is no absolutely right way to respond to an offer.

However, it is best to begin with some rudimentary improv games before thinking about more detailed scene work, to build confidence and to get them used to listening to each other and responding to each other.

Here are three activities to begin with: (Remember: they can be done one group at a time or with several groups at the same time.)

Activity What Are You Doing?

What Are You Doing? is usually done as a single group exercise (but there are no laws about this). Have the group form one big circle. Ask for a volunteer to go to the centre of the circle and give him a physical activity to mime, for example, "brushing my teeth." Your volunteer then pretends to brush his or her teeth. Once the action is clear, after about five to ten seconds, another person enters the centre of the circle and asks the "tooth brusher", "What are you doing?" The first volunteer answers with another activity that has nothing to do with brushing teeth. For example, "Washing my dog". The new person then begins to pretend to wash her dog as the first person returns to his place in the circle. Work your way around the circle until everyone has had a chance to be in the centre.

Activity Word at a Time

In **Word at a Time**, divide a larger group into smaller groups of six to eight and have them sit in circles, keeping the groups as far away from each other as possible (so they can hear themselves better). The groups are going to tell a short story, with a beginning, a middle and an end by having each person in the group say one word at a time. To begin, choose a volunteer in each group. That person will offer one word (for example, *Once*). The person to their left or right, which would be predetermined, will add the next word (for example, *upon*). As kids get more comfortable with the exercise, eliminate "Once upon a time" as a way of starting a story.

Have a new volunteer begin with a new word (for example, *After*) and see where the story goes. For a variation you can have them try and tell a very short narrative with a beginning, a middle, and an end by going around the circle three times. Warn the group that this means each word must be chosen carefully. Just so you know, it is very common for characters to die and come back to life or to throw up, but that will pass as confidence grows! You can adapt this game to your own preferences based on your group's comfort level and expertise.

Activity Questions Only

Questions Only is a game that is exactly what it sounds like. When you speak you can only ask questions. To begin, divide the larger group into smaller groups of eight or ten. Then divide each of those groups in half and have them form two single lines facing each other six or eight feet apart so that the first people on each 'team' are facing each other and the rest of each team is lined up behind them.

Give the whole group a topic (so they will start without overthinking). In each pair of teams, decide which team will start. You can simply say, "A's will start this round." The first person in each line will step forward and the person from team A will ask a question. Any question is appropriate, as long as it relates to the topic they have been given. For example, if the topic was "school" that person might ask. . . .

"Do you like school?"

The first person in line B must now answer right way with another question, such as. . . .

"How far do you have to walk to get here?"

When someone makes a mistake, such as by starting to answer a question, or by hesitating before beginning to answer or by asking the same question back, that person goes to the back of their line and the next person steps forward to continue the question process. You can decide whether the new person begins the questioning or if the person remaining in place from the opposite team begins. The temptation to answer to some degree is very strong in all us, so let them know they will all do that at some point. This is a very good concentration exercise and a lot of fun to play, for anyone.

With repetition, they will improve pretty quickly—which brings me to another point: all of these games can be played more than once. Changing the makeup of the groups and lowering response time will help keep things fresh. It's more challenging than it sounds, especially when the pace picks up.

These three games are just a sample of a very large number of games or exercises for kids available online or in improv books. Many websites will give you a sense of the age range the games apply to. The following websites are three to explore:

- www.improvencyclopedia.org (Encyclopedia of Improv Games)
- www.improv.ca/training (Canadian Improv Games)
- www.learnimprov.com (The Art of Improvisational Comedy Theatre)

A simple search online will garner many clearly explained games. Start slowly and you will build up a repertoire surprisingly fast. Once kids have some basic listening and responding skills, they can start to do some simple scene work.

A closing word: Some adults have expressed a little reluctance to try improv because they are worried about what kids might say in a scene. It may be language choice or the topics they want to bring up in front of their peers. . . .usually sex or drug related. This is generally a "teenager" issue, but it is not difficult to deal with. . . .honest.

When you begin scene work, let them know right off the top that scene work will be 'family show' only. Say to the kids: "If you wouldn't want your grandmother to watch the scene, then don't show it to the group." If a scene begins to go in an unsuitable direction—and nerves can be a big contributing factor to where scenes go when kids are new to performing improv—stop the scene right away with something like: "Thank you. Family show. Next scene." or "Thank you. Family show. Let's start the scene again." Move on to the next scene right away.

Apply the "AT&T test": appropriate, timely and tasteful.

If a scene becomes racist or politically incorrect, use it as a teachable moment to talk about being sensitive to differences.

Encourage children to go for the interesting, not the shocking. Shock value can be attractive at a certain age, but the scenes that go for shock value are very predictable as there is nowhere to go with them. The key is for you to be consistent from the outset. Students will deal with it, and the work will be better and more fun in the long run.

Clowns:

theatrical clowns, class clowns, therapeutic and circus clowns

In many ways, kids understand clowning already just because they are kids. They are already clown-like and can teach adults a lot about play through their natural approach to life. Research tells us that 93 percent of all communication is nonverbal. So physical comedy with few or no real words has broad appeal to people of all ages, especially those who don't speak English.

Helen Donnelly, a founding member of the Canadian Association of Therapeutic Clowns, has been teaching clown and movement workshops for nearly ten years in and around Toronto, Canada, and has performed with *Cirque du Soleil,* among other performance groups, in live comedic interaction with audiences. She also runs her own theatrical clown company, *Foo Productions.* I was a student of Helen's for two summers at the Haliburton School of the Arts, in Ontario, Canada. In a recent conversation with her, she explained that "kids aren't old enough to have the life experiences to be a clown. One definition of clowning is 'life after experience' and kids don't have it, so it would be an insult to the art form and to kids to teach them to be clowns. Having said that, kids are already clownlike in their innocence and youth. They can appreciate clowning as an art form and learn more about it."

Theatrical clowning is improvised. There may be a script or a general outline, but the clown improvises within the performance and stays in the present with the audience. For instance, if someone sneezes in the audience, a clown would never let it go unnoticed. The clown in a live theatre performance would stop and acknowledge the sneeze with a gesture offering a tissue or a genuine look of surprise and concern for the sneezer. Theatrical clowns are based on characters with accompanying costumes and props. They don't wear white painted faces as circus clowns do. They wear makeup to accentuate their character. They may speak English or use their own gibberish language to communicate their humour. Developing these characters can take years.

Here are two examples of theatrical clowns in scripted TV comedy who use their body and emotions to communicate an idea and build a story or a playful interaction as well as dialogue.

a) *Cosmo Kramer* played by Michael Richards on the TV sitcom *Seinfeld* with his simple and honest, slapstick gestures
b) *Byron "Buster" Bluth* played by Tony Hale on the TV comedy *Arrested Development* is 100 percent clown.

Fast-paced slapstick is part of clowning: pratfalls, exaggerated physical activities, mishaps and accidents that often look violent (but aren't). It is one of the hardest forms of comedy to perform because it requires split-second timing even though it may look easy.

Children love to watch clowning styles and learn more about clowning through Kramer and older classic clowns such as Buster Keaton, Charlie Chaplin, Laurel and Hardy, Lucille Ball, Jerry Lewis, Red Skelton and Peter Sellers.

Jim Carrey is Canada's most famous clown actor. Director Tom Shadyac, (who was introduced in Part One in connection with the film *Happy*) thinks Jim Carrey's appeal has a lot to do with remaining in touch with the kid in himself and the kid in all of us. "I look at [him] as being childlike," he says, "because children, as you know, can go from zero to hero in a second. Jim has that, embodies that child. And so I think it's cathartic for us to see Jim, to watch his movies, because it gets us back in touch with our sense of youth. I think future generations will look back on him, and maybe he's sort of the pinnacle of those physically gifted comics."—Joel Garner, 2004, p.142.

Experience Jim's acting and clown skills in movies such as *Ace Ventura: Pet Detective, The Mask, Liar, Liar* and *Dumb and Dumber.*

Teachers and parents may want to take a course in clowning to remind themselves of the importance of being light and playful in their work and in life in general and to discover their own clown persona. As Donnelly says, learning the craft of clown consists of three parts:

a. Taking workshops

b. Performing in cabarets/showcases/fundraisers/etc., and

c. Seeing clown shows

Therapeutic Medical Clowns

Being hurt or sick in a hospital is a scary experience for children. Many innovative hospitals and rehabilitation centers have introduced therapeutic clowns to interact with children and their families through spontaneous play and humour to reduce the stress and fear of the hospital experience. Their communication is more nonverbal than verbal because the children are hospitalized for a variety of physical or cognitive issues, such as brain injuries, physical disabilities or operations. The presence of a clown in the room can be a useful distraction when a child is having a medical procedure or physiotherapy.

Therapeutic clowns work as part of the team of nurses, doctors, physiotherapists and psychologists to help children adjust to the reality of the unknown noises, equipment and procedures in a hospital room. While medical staff can come and go, the clown develops an ongoing relationship as a friend and playmate.

Helen Donnelly is a founding member of the Canadian Association of Therapeutic Clowns. Her website shares this statement, "Her passion in the therapeutic clown field includes raising standards of practice and involving herself in research efforts to bring about a better understanding of this alternative arts-based practice on clients."

Nurse Polo and Dr. Flap
—Photo used with permission from Helen Donnelly

Using skills including music, rhythm, movement, physical comedy and slapstick, Nurse Polo and Dr. Flap provide warmth and laughter to clients, families and staff.—Holland Bloorview Kids Rehabilitation Centre in Toronto, featuring therapeutic clowns Helen Donnelly (a founding member) and Manuel Rodriguez.

A Famous Clown Doctor

The category of therapeutic clowns wouldn't be complete without the inclusion of Dr. Hunter "Patch" Adams. Many people are familiar with the movie about him featuring Robin Williams, *Patch Adams M.D.* There is much more to this radical, revolutionary man and his lifelong work in what he would call "humanitarian clowning" than any movie could capture. He is dedicated to helping people around the world envision a much more inclusive type of holistic medicine, healing and hospitals than we experience now. His model integrates medicine with performing arts, arts and crafts, agriculture, nature education and social service.

In addition to the technical skills they learn, Patch believes that doctors need much more training in compassion, love and caring. He views the whole world as a caring hospital and makes regular outreach trips to Costa Rica, Peru and Russia and special visits to Kabul, Afghanistan where he and his team use a combination of building, teaching, learning and play. Together, they "clown" in hospitals, care facilities, prisons, hospices and other care facilities.

His model is organized around these principles:

- Care is free.
- Patients are treated as friends.
- Ample time is given to the care interaction (for example, initial interviews with patients are three hours long).
- All complementary medicine is welcomed.
- The health of the staff is as important as the health of the patients.
- Care is infused with fun and play.

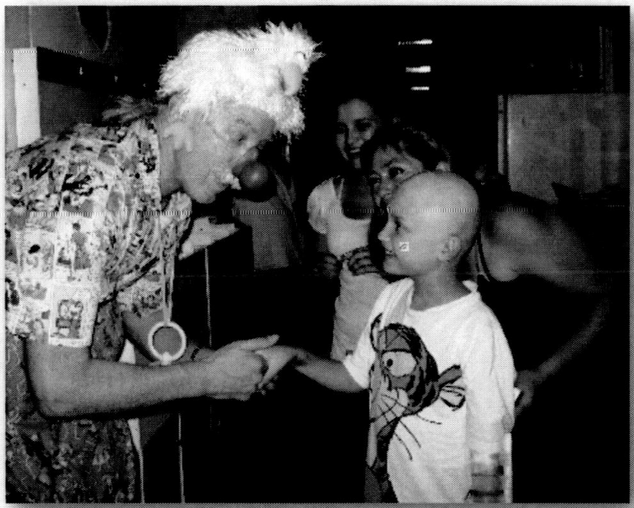

Dr. Patch Adams greets a child and family.

—Photo used with permission from Dr. Patch Adams

Dr. Patch Adams founded the Gesundheit! Institute as a not-for-profit health care organization. In its forty-year history, Gesundheit has offered care to tens of thousands, given workshops and lectures in over sixty-five countries, built and supported clinics, schools, and orphanages from El Salvador to Cambodia and brought the joy of clowning to parts of the world damaged by violence and injustice.

Circus Clowns

Circus clowns with masks made from face paint, large clown shoes, baggy clothes, wigs and brightly coloured, outlandish costumes entertain audiences with their antics and gags in the big tents at circuses, arenas, rodeos and local fairs. They can be happy or sad clowns based on their makeup. The best ones are masters of physical comedy in facial expression, slapstick movements and use of juggling and magic tricks.

As a cautionary note, I must add that some children and adults are afraid of clowns, so be ready for a variety of reactions. You may want to invite a clown to visit your class or stop with your child and talk when you see a street clown or performer in a public place. In order for children to relax and enjoy the clowning, it's important for children to understand that it's a clown's purpose to make people smile and giggle.

Emmett Kelly, the famous Ringling Brothers clown, was so skilled in pantomiming the role of Weary Willie that he was allowed to remain in the circus arena through the entire performance. His most famous act was to sweep a circle of light thrown by a spotlight into a smaller and smaller circle, and then to chase it under a rug or into a dustbin.

The World's Smallest Mask

The red clown nose is an integral part of the clown's costume and is known as the world's smallest mask. On its own, this little red sponge ball can communicate happiness and bring a smile to all. For a clown to put on the red nose, he or she must be in character until the nose is removed—it's that powerful.

One day at a conference I was attending, Allen Klein gave everyone in the audience a small envelope. He asked people to close their eyes and think about something that was upsetting them. Then he asked us to open the envelope and put on the red clown nose that was inside, and look at everybody around the room. We all burst into laughter at the site of all the red clown noses on all the smiling faces.

Allen told us about a mother who wears a red clown nose to get her kids out of bed on school mornings. A practice I have adopted from Allen is to keep a clown nose in my car and when I get into a traffic jam, I put it on and glance at neighbouring drivers with a big smile. Try this yourself in different locations. Everyone laughs—and relaxes.

Note: A source for inexpensive red clown noses in bulk is:
Rhode Island Novelty, tel.1-800-528-5599, www.rinovelty.com

Class Clowns

> *"The forbidden is always funny. The funniest word in the vocabulary of a second grader is "underwear". —Betsy Byars, author*

In a typical group of thirty kids, there will usually be one who jokes around and keeps everyone laughing—the class clown. A teacher will be in the middle of a complex lesson asking a pivotal question and—WHAMO—the class clown interjects with a witty wisecrack of an answer. Everyone laughs and looks at the class clown, and the teacher momentarily loses the attention of the class. These clowns can make teachers shudder in fear of the havoc they can wreak on carefully planned lessons and the distraction they are to classmates. Some teachers react angrily and reprimand the child, losing their train of thought and probably their own composure, both at the same time. I believe that most class clowns are misunderstood.

Wise teachers see class clowns in a positive light. They use strategies to appreciate and honour the spontaneous humour and joy-filled playfulness of the class clown (much more likely to be male) and encourage that comedic intelligence in more constructive directions. They build a workable and playable relationship over time for everyone concerned. Parents and teachers know that a bubbly funprint (sense of humour) is a characteristic to be desired in children. We nurture this kind of funprint outside of school, so there should be a suitable place for it to shine in a healthy, fun-loving learning classroom.

Popular children's literature writer Robert Munsch wrote *Class Clown* in 2007 and dedicated it to a boy called Leonardo. Munsch writes: "Leonardo has been funny ever since he was a baby. When his teacher asks him not to make all the kids in the class laugh anymore, he tries and tries. . . .but he just can't help being the class clown!"

In William Purkey's book *Teaching Class Clowns (and what they can teach us)*, he writes that the contributions of class clowns, "have been totally neglected in the professional education literature. Hundreds of books, if not thousands, have been written about gifted and talented students. A similar number have been written about children with special needs. Yet almost nothing has been written on how to understand class clowns and appreciate their contributions."—Purkey. 2006. p. x. He conducted a large-scale research study of class clowns at the University of Florida with a colleague Dr. Sandra Damico involving ninety-six class clowns from 3,500 eighth grade classes. They found that class clowns:

- Demonstrate a pattern of rebellion and nonconformity
- Do have a respect for feelings of others
- Are not timid
- Are often outsiders
- Although not academic stars at school, class clowns possess a curious mind, quick intelligence, dexterity of thought and a huge funny bone.

Often class clowns use humour to cope with challenges they faced as children. They may have had to live with parents who rejected them, who fought a lot or ended up in divorce. Some grew up in poverty and homelessness. Perhaps because of these challenges, these kids are more likely to be creative and verbally intelligent, and feel no fear when performing in front of groups. Parents and teachers can work together to support the development of these especially funny kids.

If teachers and parents include humour, and they themselves have a visible sense of humour with kids, then unwanted interruptions from kids will be easier for everyone to enjoy. Consider these tips to treat class clowns with dignity, include them and give them positive attention when they do burst forth with quick one-liners or hilarious quips or actions.

- Acknowledge the funny comment with a friendly wink and eye contact.
- Move closer to the student.
- Pause to have a laugh with everyone and admit it is funny.
- Quickly return to the activity you were doing.

Teachers can channel in a positive way the many skills of class clowns by using these strategies:
- Allow shared responsibility by soliciting their help.
- Encourage them to use their talents on the morning announcements.
- Assign them leadership positions so they can be seen in a different way.
- Organize talent shows that can showcase their skills.
- Schedule time each day or week for kids to share funny stories.
- Have a class discussion about the role of humour during classes and at school.

"At the beginning of the school year she was standing by her classroom welcoming new students when Johnny, a bright-eyed kindergartener, asked the teacher which seat he should take. She motioned to her classroom and replied, "Just go on in and take any seat you like." Several minutes later she entered the classroom and found Johnny comfortably settled in the teacher's chair located behind her desk. He had his pencils, paper and lunchbox neatly laid out and was ready for his first day of school."
—Purkey, 2006, p. 51. [a story told by Diane Jones, a kindergarten teacher]

Play Signals

Develop nonthreatening warning signals to shift gears if kids get carried away. Let kids know there will be a time to return to and appreciate these saved-up funnies. Here are some methods you could try:

- clapping your hands
- raising your hand
- squeezing a bicycle horn
- ringing a bell

Note: The final section in Part Two, That's Not Funny, provides strategies to help kids understand the differences between hurtful and helpful humour. It's a different story when class clowns are hostile or mean and teasing escalates into hurtful bullying.

Build Relationships

One sure way to work with a class clown is to share the stage with him or her at times. A few years ago, a teacher at a workshop shared a brilliant idea with several of us. She knew she had a budding comedian in her grade 10 class. One day she made some time to sit down with him and explain his effect on the class and her lessons. She made him an offer he couldn't refuse—ten minutes each Friday to recap the week in his own way. The result of this deal was that he stayed more focused during the week and benefited from testing his jokes on a very willing audience. Many comedians, including Jim Carrey, had similar stories to tell about a special teacher who connected with them in high school.

Budding Comedians

When I ask teachers to explain why they chose education as a career, many of them tell elaborate stories of playing teacher when they were children. They gathered kids from around their neighbourhood and organized their own "classroom" somewhere in their house with paper and pens for all! Comedians share the same early feelings of their life-calling as young children.

Consider the genius of these comedians—Jonathan Winters, Robin Williams, Jay Leno, Jim Carrey and Joan Rivers. They each tell stories about developing their comic skills early in life. Purkey found that in virtually every case, professional comedians began their careers as class clowns. Here are a few examples he cites (p. 13):

- Bob Hope demonstrated his remarkable ability to make people laugh by the time he was four years of age.
- Tim Conway was breaking classmates up in kindergarten.
- Jerry Seinfeld was writing a book about humour while he was still a young boy.

Whether out of boredom or because of learning challenges that precluded concentration, they discovered that making their friends laugh earned them approval and attention. They had a built-in audience every single day.

Visit www.suswb.ca to learn more about a Canadian program called Stand UP for Student Well Being (formerly Happiness at School) that uses comedy to promote literacy and mental health.

Activity Start a Kids' Comedy Club

Many schools have public speaking contests or trivia contests and spelling bees. Set aside time during the week for kids to share their funprints with jokes and stories. For example, Tuesdays could become Tickle Your Funny Bone Tuesday!

Consider adding a comedy club to the opportunities kids have to perform in front of others. Kids could sign up for a club that meets weekly, or meet for five or six sessions leading up to a performance. Activities from this book would be ideal starting points to set the stage for kids to practise telling jokes or doing improv. Encourage them to write their own material, use their own personality and work up short sketches or skits. Practising with each other will be a useful way to master the written material and hone their timing and delivery.

> William J. Smart wrote about his granddaughter Madeline's first day in grade 1 in a story he wrote for *The Toronto Star* called "Kids Have It Easier These Days". One day she explained with delight how grade 1 would be different. The new school bag will cover her back completely, real homework will be assigned. "Times have changed, grandpa," she says. "Anyway, I'm 6 now. Heck, I waited years for this."

Activity Class Clown Debate

Hold a discussion or debate in class on this topic: "Do class clowns play an important role in creating a better learning environment in school?"

Melbourne International Comedy Festival

Australians celebrate the skills of class clowns with a competition, now in its eleventh year, for secondary school students fourteen to eighteen years old. "Each year hundreds of. . .students participate in the competition across the country —discovering or refining their skills in writing and performing comedy and channelling all that cheeky tomfoolery into entertainment for a wider audience." It's free to enter and the winner gets prize money for him or herself and for the school.

- They have five minutes for their sketch (skit).
- There can be up to three people in each group.
- Routines must be original, well rehearsed (and funny).
- Sketch acts, stand-up, parody and musical comedy are all welcome.

On their website, teachers note the added benefits of the crash-course workshop that is offered before the competition—ongoing development of problem solving and collaborative and public speaking skills. Here is a comment from Susan Cole, Melbourne Girls' College: "Our Comedy unit has become a highlight of the Year 9 school year for not only the students and teachers but also the parents and the wider community. Developing their own comedy act is a chance for our students to articulate their ideas and understandings in effect creating their own social commentary of the world in which they live."

Class clowns can teach us all lessons about happiness, humour and laughter, and adults can teach them valuable lessons too!

Stand-Up Comedians

Comedy is a dynamic art that relies on a constant stream of talent and new ideas and approaches. Current influences are having an impact on how comedy is created and presented. The explosion of the World Wide Web and sites such as YouTube can make comedy cheap and accessible for all to create, view and share. Below are brief descriptions of the various styles of comedy. Although one style may dominate in a comedian's routine or in a short or long narrative, many comedic forms combine two or more styles.

Styles of Comedy

Mime

All physical theatre comes from mime, which uses the body and emotions to communicate an idea and build a story or a playful interaction. Mime is comedy based on creating reality through actions alone. Normally people performing mime are not allowed to speak, although sound effects and sometimes the odd word are used. The challenge of mime is not just to give the impression of something happening on stage but to make it entertaining and amusing. The *Blue Man Group* is a contemporary example of mime performers.

Absurdism

Often described as "zany" or "off-the-wall" comedy, this sort of humour derives from illogical, extremely nonsensical situations so ridiculous that the gap between reality and the comic's presentation of it is glaringly obvious. The Monty Python team use this style extensively in movies such as *Monty Python's Flying Circus.*

Black or Dark Comedy

Black or dark comedy uses humour to deal with uncomfortable or painful topics such as war (*MASH*), racism (Chris Rock) and death and dying (hospital humour). Its purpose is to create distance from the pain and fear associated with life's biggest and most profound challenges.

Character Comedy

In character comedy, the performer adopts a persona (the technical word for a false identity or mask). Many performers like appearing "in character" because it gives them a sense of freedom to do and say things they wouldn't dare do as themselves. An example is the Jim Parsons character Sheldon Cooper on the TV comedy *The Big Bang Theory*.

Parody

Parody is performing an imitation of something such as a song, or a TV show, TV commercial or a film. To work, parody must not only be a good imitation but also be funny—for example, Weird Al Yankovic.

Satire

Satire is comedy with a message. It attempts to point out the flaws in something by exaggerating that flaw until it seems totally absurd. (*Saturday Night Live* is an example of a TV show based on satire.) Politicians, police and pop stars are favourite targets. It is the most "intellectual" form of comedy and has always been popular among young people who want to make fun of authority figures.

Slapstick

Slapstick derives from physical circus clowning and was popular in the early days of vaudeville. It involved carefully set up sight gags, including lots of falls and exploding props. An example is the character Kramer in *Seinfeld*.

Stand-Up Comedy

Stand-up comedy is most often performed by a single person standing up in front of an audience. Some stand-ups just tell jokes. Others do monologues, which are longer discussions about particular topics. Some do observation comedy based on talking about funny things in life, like Jerry Seinfeld or Bill Cosby. There are many variations on stand-up comedy including puppeteers and ventriloquists.

Some comedians work in pairs, with one person being the straight or serious man or woman and the other the fool. The straight man tries to have a serious conversation but always gets nonsensical answers or is misunderstood by his partner. Probably the most famous example of this pattern is the routine by Abbot and Costello called "Who's on First?" (Double acts rely on well-rehearsed pieces called "routines" or short plays called "sketches".) Groups or teams of performers are called "ensembles".

—Based on *Are You Trying to Be Funny?* Used by permission from Melbourne International Comedy Festival—Class Clowns by Ian McFadyen, Updated in 2011 by Karin Farrell, Producer, Education and Development Programs.

Activity Styles of Comedy

Use the chart that follows to collect a record of various styles of comedy. Remember, styles may be combined in all sorts of different ways. You might see a double act that performs mime or an ensemble who performs as a range of different characters.

Think of some comedy movies and TV shows that make you laugh. Why are they funny to you? Maybe you like *Toy Story* or *Monsters Inc.* Have a look at some old comedies like *I Love Lucy, Laurel and Hardy*, and a British favourite, *Fawlty Towers*, and talk about why they are funny to get you started on your own writing. Watch for their comic sense of timing and delivery.

- Which style of comedy do you like to experience the most?
- Which comedians are your favourites?
- Which styles are closest to your personal sense of humour or funprint?

STYLE OF COMEDY	Examples	Personal Reactions
Absurdism		
Character Comedy		
Mime		
Parody		
Satire		
Slapstick		
Stand-Up		

Activity: Stand-Up Comedians Through the Years

Use the following chart format to start making a list of comedians. Kids can add to the chart and categorize them as they experience more stand-up comedians.

Classic	Current	Up and Coming
Lucille Ball	Tina Fey	Seth Rogen
Abbott & Costello	Steve Carrell	Jonah Hill
Red Skelton	Whoopi Goldberg	Johnny Galecki
Mary Tyler Moore	Ellen DeGeneres	Kaley Cuoco
	Jim Carrey	Jim Parsons
		Mayim Bialik
		Melissa Rauch

Comedy as a Coping Mechanism

Like clowns, many comedians found doing well at school very difficult for them, or they were bullied as kids, or both. They learned to use humour to cope with school and find fun in their lives.

"Overall then, although research does not support the popular view that professional comedians are depressed or otherwise psychologically disturbed, it does suggest that humour in these individuals serves as a defense or coping mechanism for dealing with adversity in early life."
—Martin, 2007. p. 225

Comedy actor and producer Jim Carrey is an example. He was born in Ontario, Canada, and is the youngest of four children. His family struggled through a period of tragic financial difficulty and moved into a camper van at one point in his childhood. He dropped out of high school and worked as a janitor. It is said that he performed constantly as a child—for anyone who would watch. He was a straight A student until he dropped out.

Here's what comedian Jay Leno said when asked, "Were you good in school?" "*Knowing the answer in class didn't come easy to me. I was dyslexic, so school was never my favorite place. I was especially terrible in math. I used to put my hand up in class and ask my teacher, 'Where did mathematics come from?' He would turn red. 'You're not fooling anyone, Mr. Leno. Your annoying question is intended to take us off the subject; you don't care where mathematics came from!' The same teacher once wrote on my report card, 'If Jay spent as much time studying as he did trying to be a comedian, he'd be a star.' That confuses me to this day. How was I going to become a star without trying to be a comedian?"*—Jay Leno. 2005.

Observational Humour

Comedians use observational humour, always aware of the funny things going on around them. Here are some hints to share with young comedians as they perfect their delivery skills and adept timing.

Keep a notebook with you to collect ideas. Write your joke collection down on file cards or in your notebook—or even in your computer—so you can practise and perfect them.

Take advantage of social situations to try out your material such as standing in the line at the movies, eating in the lunchroom with your friends, or talking with waitresses in a restaurant.

All through my high school, I worked at McDonald's. Believe it or not, my job flipping burgers was responsible for my career in comedy. McDonald's put on a regional talent show. My manager suggested I put together a comedy routine for the show. So I got together with a guy called Jay Monroe and came up with a routine. We won the competition and the $150 cash prize. That was the first glimmer that I could make money by telling jokes. All thanks to McDonald's. —Jay Leno, 2005. p. 49

Jay Leno—the host of *The Tonight Show* started telling jokes when he was four years old! He wrote a great book for kids—*How to Be the Funniest Kid in the World (or just in your class!)* He says, "Writing jokes is fun. Telling them is even more fun."

- Copy someone you like and borrow from them until you write your own material.
- Loosen up your funny bones by jumping up and down and acting a little crazy.
- Work your body—use your arms and hands, don't stuff them in your pockets.
- It's all in the delivery. Think about how fast or slow you are telling the joke.
- Practise using a digital voice recorder (maybe on your phone) or a pen and paper to keep a record of your ideas. Then make a list of jokes you could use to put in a routine—maybe five or six jokes. You can decide which ones to use and which ones to cut out.
- It's normal to feel stage fright or be nervous. Go out on an empty stage to practise.
- Play with the audience and have fun.
- Work on your own laugh and make it part of your act. For example, watch and listen to Phyllis Diller on YouTube.
- If you mess up, keep going because the audience doesn't know your act. (Taking a risk to be funny means that you're going to bomb or mess up. Practise on your friends before you "take it on the road" with strangers.)
- Good joke tellers can see the non-serious or funny side of a situation when they make up their punch lines—the line at the end that gets the laugh.

- Don't forget the punch line above all else. From it, you should be able to go back and recreate the joke if you forget some of the details.

While you can be funny just on your own, you can always use props like funny noses, weird lips, costumes, stuffed animals that talk, balloons and bubbles. You can shop for these items in novelty stores or order them online. See if using props suits your style as a comedian, or if you would rather go prop-less!

> *"MickeyMinniePlutoHueyLouieDeweyDonaldGoofySacramento"*
> *When asked why a teenage girl had such a long password, she rolled her eyes and said, "Hello! It has to be at least eight characters long and include at least one capital."*

Activity . . . What Would Your Comedy Act Be?

Many comics write and perform their own material. But some have a team of writers to write some or all of their jokes. It will take the writers hours or days to come up with jokes for a short monologue, a longer routine or a thirty-minute sitcom.

- Use some of the warm-up activities in the section on improv.
- Then, in pairs or triads, let kids test out their comedic skills by writing their own comedy sketch.
- Ask kids to brainstorm their ideas for the sketch and decide what type/style of comedy their sketch will be.
- Encourage them to keep the sketch short (no more than a minute) and not too complicated.
- Plan the characters, dialogue, setting and props (if being used).
- Have the kids rehearse and refine their sketch, then perform it in front of everyone or in smaller groups.

Following the performances, ask them to reflect with their partners or class members on these questions:

- What worked well with the comedy sketch?
- What changes would you make and why?

Encourage them to revise the sketch and keep on perfecting it until they are happy with it.

—from the Australian Broadcasting Corporation, ABC, *Behind the News*, March 2012.

Kids could perform against other schools and communities. Judges could be a combination of local comedians, community -college comedy teachers, Toastmasters International—and parents.

Students may be inspired to know that there are college courses they can enroll in when they graduate from high school to continue learning about comedy. An example is Humber College in Toronto. This writing and performance program helps talented students hone their craft while gaining an understanding of the commercial side of the industry. Students learn stand-up, sketch comedy, scriptwriting and other aspects of the craft.

Adults need to be reminded that kids in the same family or in the same class will each have their own unique sense of humour or funprint. It's such a personal thing. We must recognize, develop and celebrate these differences.

A man tells his doctor, "Doc, help me. I'm addicted to Twitter."
The doctor replies, "Sorry, I don't follow you. . . ."

That's Not Funny

Just as there are two sides to every coin, humour can also have two sides: the good and the bad. You have read about the good side of humour. The flip side is humour that is nasty and cruel. Sometimes people try to be funny and have fun at the expense of others. This hurtful humour is a form of bullying that, like other forms, needs to be confronted and discussed so that kids can develop strategies to deal with it.

Humour: Two Sides of the Coin

Consider these two lists of words for the two sides of humour. What other descriptors would you add?

Healthy	**Unhealthy**
appropriate	inappropriate
happy	hurtful
optimistic	pessimistic
positive	negative, cynical
sensitive	offensive, sadistic
playful	aggressive, threatening
safe	hostile, toxic
feels better	feels worse, put downs
warm	humiliating
inviting	demeaning, cruel

Activity: It's Healthy Humour When

Distribute three or four sticky notes in two colours to each child. Ask them to write on one colour note how they would know if a humourous comment is a healthy one.

On the other colour, students write how they would know if the comment is unhealthy.

For example:
Healthy humour raises self-esteem and includes people.
Unhealthy humour lowers self-esteem and excludes people.

Here is a chance to teach a rule of humour that all kids should learn. You can laugh WITH almost anyone. The only person you can safely laugh AT is yourself. Laughing at the expense of someone's feelings is never funny.

Activity • Discuss America's Funniest Home Video

Many viewers find AFHV to be a truly funny TV show. However, when it isn't about animals, it is based on laughing at people who either unintentionally or intentionally hurt themselves or do stupid or embarrassing things.

Ask students what their opinion is of this TV show now that they know the difference between healthy and unhealthy humour. What are the differences in the video clips they show each week? Do the winning clips have a more healthy humour to them?

"Happy" Violence

Sometimes crowd violence breaks out during or after highly competitive sports events. For example, riots broke out at the end of the Stanley Cup final hockey game in 2011 in Vancouver. What was particularly disturbing about the images that emerged from that incident was the number of people who seemed to be smiling and having fun as they rampaged through the streets smashing windows, looting stores and burning cars. Some of this alienation and disregard for personal and public property can be traced to the pervasiveness of media violence. Media critic George Gerbner called it an "acceptance of 'happy violence', violence that engenders laughter and 'good times', while desensitizing viewers to the deep pain and suffering violence entails."

—*Rioting and the culture of violence* by Stephen Bede Scharper, Toronto Star, June 20, 2011.

This "happy violence" seen in a rioting crowd is similar to the glee and excitement shared by a person who bullies and the people who observe bullying and do nothing to help.

Practical Jokes

Practical joking usually involves playing funny tricks on others either with words or outrageous actions. April Fool's Day (April 1st) has become a traditional occasion for practical jokes. These jokes can cross the line of respect and fun to become cruel and embarrassing. Adults need to prepare younger kids for this day so they know what to expect and so they can discuss what might be appropriately funny but not hurtful. Use April 1st to mark the first day of National Humour Month each year and as an opportunity to focus on healthy humour.

When Teasing Becomes Bullying

Teasing is a normal aspect of a healthy relationship if it's communicated in a warm and friendly manner. Sometimes a comment made in jest is misinterpreted as a criticism or put-down. These mistakes in communication can be corrected. This is why sarcasm (a sneering or cutting remark) is so hurtful to use unless there is a strong relationship in place. Some people are more sensitive and may not be able to tell when a friend is teasing in a sarcastic way. Are they being mean or just having fun? Very close friends can say negative things to each other in fun and no one feels hurt. They know there is no harm in it.

On the other hand, if the comment is truly hurtful, the target feels embarrassed and humiliated in front of others. They feel "diss-ed" or disrespected. Unhealthy and aggressive teasing becomes bullying if the intention is to upset or hurt.

The challenge for kids is to know that all teasing isn't fun. It can turn into taunting and become bullying.

This definition of bullying, used by the Ministry of Education in Ontario, Canada, forms the basis of a safe school plan to teach students and teachers about bullying and bullying prevention:

"Bullying is typically a form of repeated, persistent or aggressive behaviour directed at an individual or individuals that is intended to cause (or should be known to cause) fear and distress and/or harm to another person's body, feelings, self-esteem and reputation. Bullying occurs in a context where there is a real or perceived power imbalance."

—Policy/Program Memorandum No. 144, Oct. 19, 2009.

When young people bully others, inflicting emotional or physical pain gives them a form of satisfaction, even if it's only temporary. They may be seeking attention and power, or they think it will increase their popularity. Their "humour" is often racist, sexist, or homophobic. They make fun of weaknesses and differences and often brush their cruelty off with a comment like, "I was just having some fun! It was a joke!" or "What's the matter? Can't you take a joke? I was only teasing."

The Roles of People Who Observe Bullying

"I used to make fun of this girl cuz others did. The day I apologized was the day they stopped bullying her."

—A comment on *Kids Help Phone* website

Instead of being part of the problem and laughing or looking away, people who observe bullying can be a major part of the solution to the problem. They can take a stand and:

- Refuse to laugh AT other people
- Reach out and help people who experience bullying
- Speak up and tell the person who bullies to make different choices

Strategies for Kids Who Experience Bullying to Consider

It's a worrisome task to figure out strategies that might work to help kids and their families when people laugh at them or beat them up. We have to understand that bullying is never right. It takes courage, but people who experience bullying need to reach out and tell someone.

Every strategy involves an element of risk. Above all, kids who experience bullying need to aim to stay safe and remember there is nothing wrong with them. No one ever deserves to be bullied by any other kid or adult. Here are some strategies to use in response to a person who bullies:

- Decide if it's friendly teasing or aggressive teasing.
- Travel with a friend or a group of friends.
- Avoid situations where you might meet the person, if you can.
- Hold your head up and be proud. Try to calm yourself inside and look confident outside.

- Don't look afraid or lose your temper if you can possibly do that under the circumstances.
- Use this book to help you feel good about yourself.
- Use a notebook or journal to write your feelings down.
- Try a humourous comeback line. (See further notes in the following sections.)

Comeback Lines

One idea that is mentioned briefly in resources on bullying is to use a humourous comeback line to diffuse the taunt, distract the person who bullies, take back power and leave the scene gracefully. The use of this strategy will depend on the child's personality and level of comfort. Think of it as similar to how a comedian would deal with a heckler in the audience to turn around a hostile comment—a wacky element of surprise.

In this way, the child who experiences bullying retains his or her power and shows some assertiveness in dealing with the child who bullies. While it's okay to answer back and make an unexpected comment, you don't want kids to make it worse by making fun of a person who bullies.

In his book *Kids Who Laugh*, Louis Franzini suggested this response to someone who is being physically intimidating: "Yes, you really are bigger and stronger than me. That is why I am making you my official bodyguard. This is quite an honour."

The following are more examples to consider:
- "You're really good at this. Congrats!"
- "Eureka—you've figured out I'm different from you!"
- "Using ME for laughs again, eh!"

Activity: Role Play Comeback Lines

Set the stage of a teasing situation where a person who bullies is making fun of someone. Assign the students to write some comeback lines to use to break the tension of the moment. It may work to use a self-effacing tone (not drawing attention to yourself), poke a little fun at yourself and use an element of surprise. Maybe a joke would work if its tone is playful. It's hard for any person who bullies to stay angry if she or he is laughing.

Role play some scenarios to rehearse the lines, tone of voice and the body language. Role play with an adult they trust or call *Kids Help Phone* and role play with a professional counsellor.

Ask the students if they think funny comeback lines are a realistic strategy. Could people who observe bullying use this technique to help a child who is being bullied?

The Learn to Laugh Program

*My thanks go to Tyler Morrison, comedy writer and performer, for the generous contribution of this section on his program *Learn to Laugh*.

The *Learn to Laugh* program is something that fellow comedians developed with creative director Tyler Morrison to help bring humour to schools and work with kids on how they can apply humour to their everyday lives. In this program they open up a dialogue and create a safe environment of trust with the students where they can share different experiences based on themes that we focus on during the course of the program. Below are timely comments from Morrison.

"During the bullying prevention theme in one school they discovered that one of the thirteen year old students had been constantly bullied and was having a great deal of trouble with it.

After our segment on anti-bullying he was then able to go back to school and implement humour to diffuse the verbal attacks of the students who were picking on him and gain respect from his peers."

In the case of this particular student, Tyler received an update from a mother who said she had never seen her son as confident and doing so well in school, sports, and making new friends. As much as the *Laugh to Learn* program is about humour as an important skill to instill in our young people it is also about listening to the students to identify the best way to handle different situations that may be affecting them. Every student is different. This is a great example of how a little bit of guidance and mentorship from someone can help change the lives of kids and get them to take the step from being on the outside to becoming leaders among their peers.

School can be a very primal environment, so the old saying "you can dish it out but you can't take it" very often comes into play in situations like these. When humour can be used effectively to let someone know how it feels to be on the receiving end of unwanted verbal treatment, it can serve to drive home to kids who bully that what they are doing is not pleasurable for anyone and therefore make them think twice about continuing this type of behavior in the future. The psychology of bullying can be directly compared to that of someone who goes to comedy clubs and heckles the comedians who are performing. The heckler, like a bully, seeks the attention of the group and does not know how to get it other than by attempting to put down the comedian in front of everyone in attendance. The comedian's job is to shut down the heckler through superior wit thereby turning the audience on the heckler. Their laughter and applause serves as notice to the heckler that this type of behavior is not to be tolerated by the group. Many comedians were picked on in their youth and have developed their wit as a defense mechanism. When it is utilized properly it can take someone generally viewed as an outsider and turn them into a leader.

Get Some Help

Tell students who may be experiencing bullying, " Realize that bullying is happening and get some help. Find someone trustworthy. Tell your mom, dad or a teacher or guidance counsellor you respect. Try the assistant principal, the principal or the superintendent. Call your school trustee and the school board chair if you need to go higher in the organization. Tell a friend or an older sister or brother about what's happening. If one person doesn't help, try someone else until you find the right one."

Activity — Search Sources of Help on Bullying

Assign the group to go online together to search for advice and try the many activities on *Kids' Help Phone* website: www.kidshelpphone.ca

Kids Help Phone—Toll Free 1-800-668-6868—Canada's only free, national, bilingual, confidential and anonymous, 24-hour telephone and online counselling service. They also have online services—young people can contact *Kids Help Phone* by phone, or if they feel more comfortable writing in about their problem, they can send a post on the Ask Us Online forum, or they can Live Chat with a counsellor. (Visit www.kidshelphone.ca to learn more including when Live Chat is offered—currently during half the week in the evenings with plans for further expansion of services.)

1800 668 6868
KidsHelpPhone.ca
Kids Help Phone

Listed below are other excellent sources of material and resources for kids, families, educators and other care providers on bullying:

- *The CSSN* (The Canadian Safe School Network) www.canadiansafeschools.ca 1-416-977-1050
- *PREVNet* (Promoting Relationships and Eliminating Violence Network) www.prevnet.ca Toll Free 1-866-372-2495
- Boys Town International 1-800-448-3000
- Covenant House Youth Crisis Line 1-800-999-9999

Turn Around Kids Who Bully

While the goal is to stop bullying, it's important to recognize that often underneath their outward bravado kids who bully are unhappy with their own lives and hurt inside. They are often troubled because of their current or early life experiences and need help themselves. Some kids are bullied by their own parents or other adults in their family.

In some cases, any tendency of class clowns toward hostility can be neutralized by a compassionate adult. When kids who bully others find an adult or a friend they can trust and who tries to understand them, their sense of fear diminishes.

Activity The Three R's of Relationships

Have a discussion about respect by looking at these three universal rules or norms of behaviour in positive relationships —attributed to the Dalai Lama. Everyone has the right to be treated with respect.

- Respect for yourself—for example, by speaking up if you need help or when you are being treated unfairly
- Respect for others—for example, by being careful to honour differences among people
- Respect for your actions—for example, by being responsible for your choices in what you say and do

Give an example of each one and then brainstorm other examples with the group.

Talk about what the group should do if someone breaks the Three R's. How will that person share his or her ideas with the group? Are apologies enough? Can a disrespectful action or comment be forgiven? How can the trust in a broken relationship be rebuilt?

Two Adults Who Were Bullied

Dav Pilkey is the author of the *Captain Underpants* series of books for kids. His books make kids laugh and have sold over fifty million copies around the world. He writes and illustrates his books and is now part of the Scholastic "Reading Gives you Superpowers" campaign. In his most recent book from the series, *Tippy Tinkletrousers*, he drew inspiration for his characters from his own childhood experiences.

In a recent interview with the Toronto Star reporter Kristin Rushovy (August, 2012), Pilkey says, "My friends and I were bullied in our neighbourhood by the 'MKs'—our code word for mean kids" (and I was) "tormented by other boys for preferring reading and drawing over sports". While *Tippy Tinkletrousers* deals with younger aggressors, many of his books portray the adults as villains. "The biggest bullies in my life, however, were the principal and a few of the teachers. . . .I dealt with it the same way most kids deal with bullies: I just got through it. Everything got better eventually. . . .it just took time." Rushovy writes that Dav "hopes all kids may feel comforted by the fact that they're not alone. Bullying happens, or has happened, to many of us at one time or another."

Some parents, teachers and principals were class clowns themselves when they were kids in school. As adults they can be powerful influences on class clowns by steering them away from unhealthy humour towards more friendly humour and more positive relationships and can prevent a class clown from becoming a person who bullies to get attention.

Diagnosed with ADHD and being one of the only brown kids in a white suburban neighbourhood, comedian Russell Peters was plagued as a teenager by bullies. In his book *Call Me Russell* Peters tells the story of two high school teachers who inspired him to follow his dreams—a turning point in his life. He found success in school for the first time. He writes, "This is where teachers respected me and considered my potential for the first time, and they replaced some of my awkwardness with true confidence." Ms. Kelly taught sewing in a large room near the front of the school. Russell wasn't in her class but she let him come in the classroom, be himself and make people laugh. Fred Kolar, a world-class chef who chose to teach kids his craft, was the other memorable teacher. "In Fred's class, everyone was treated as an individual, no matter how messed up they were. . . .Above and beyond teaching us kids how to cook, Fred taught us about demeanour, about thinking about others and putting yourself in their shoes before you decide to act out or judge. That's a pretty incredible lesson to have passed along."
—Peters. 2010. p.100.

Some of the most recent reports from the United States Department of Health and Human Services unfortunately reveal that bullying programs aren't succeeding as well as expected. My hope in including the topic in this book is that if educators and parents teach kids about happiness, humour and laughter, kids will grow up with more joy and self-esteem and won't feel the need to belittle others. Their humour will be healthy and constructive.

Final Thoughts on the Happiness Line

Through the book we have examined happiness and laughter as the first two pieces of *Kidding Aorund.* Loosening up your funny bones has been the third and final piece. The following Happiness Line is worthy of one more reflection here.

We comprehend, appreciate, express and experience humor and comedy in our own ways—our unique funprint. If these personal interactions with humour and comedy are developed, there will be a tangible impact on our range on the Happiness Line as adults, and most importantly, for the kids in our lives.

10 Extremely happy (feeling ecstatic, joyous, fantastic)

9 Very happy (feeling really good, elated)

8 Pretty happy (spirits high, feeling good)

7 Mildly happy (feeling fairly good and somewhat cheerful)

6 Slightly happy (just a bit above normal)

5 Neutral (not particularly happy or unhappy)

4 Slightly unhappy (just a bit below neutral)

3 Mildly unhappy (just a bit low)

2 Pretty unhappy (somewhat "blue", spirits down)

1 Very unhappy (depressed, spirits very low)

0 Extremely unhappy (utterly depressed, completely down)

The Fordyce Emotions Survey. Michael Fordyce. *Social Indicators Research* 20,355-381. Jan. 28, 2006. Reprinted with permission from Springer Publishers.

Implementation Ideas: Loosen Up Your Funny Bones

Testing the Water

Reveal your adult funprint as you explore those of kids.

Add humour to classroom displays or home spaces.

Use funny warm-ups, transitions and cool-downs.

Keep a running journal of the funny things kids said or did.

Getting Your Feet Wet

Tell funny stories about yourself.

Encourage kids who are naturally funny to use this unique intelligence in a positive way. You may find a budding comedian in your midst.

Plan play breaks during the day with jokes and riddles.

Devise a signal or routine to pull kids back after a play break.

Jumping in the Deep End

Ask kids who are naturally funny to share their humour with others. Give them time to "perform".

Start a Comedy Club or a Kids Comedy Corner.

Use props, costumes and sound effects. Don't worry about looking silly. You will gain more points than you lose if you are lighthearted.

Teach the key messages to someone else and pay it forward.

Dig into the resources to learn more.

What implementation ideas would you add?

Resources on Humour and Comedy

Books, Magazines

Adams, Patch, with Mylander, Maureen. (1998). *Gesundheit! Bringing Good Health to You, the Medical System, and Society Through Physician Service, Complementary Therapies, Humor, and Joy*. Vermont: Healing Arts Press.

Anderson, Shona. (2011). *No More Bystanders = No More Bullies: Activating Action in Education Professionals*. CA: Corwin Press.

Berk, Ronald A. (2002). *Humor As an INSTRUCTIONAL DEFIBRILLATOR: Evidence-Based Techniques in Teaching and Assessment*. Virginia: Stylus Publishing.

Berk, Ronald A. (2003). *Professors Are from Mars. Students Are from Snickers: How to Write and Deliver Humor in the Classroom and in Professional Presentations*. Virginia: Stylus Publishing.

Brown, Stuart. (2009). *Play: How It Shapes the Brain, Opens the Imagination and Invigorates the Soul*. New York, NY: Avery.

Carter, Judy. (2001). *The Comedy Bible: From Stand-up to Sitcom—The Comedy Writer's Ultimate "How To" Guide*. New York, NY: Fireside.

Franzini, Louis. (2001). *Kids Who Laugh: How to Develop Your Child's Sense of Humor*. Garden City Park, NY: Square One Publishers.

Franzini, Louis. (2012). *Just Kidding: Using Humour Effectively*. New York, NY: Rowman & Littlefield.

Gardner, Howard. (1993). *Multiple Intelligences: The Theory in Practice*. New York, NY: Basic Books.

Gardner, Howard. (1983). *Frames of Mind: The Theory of Multiple Intelligences*. New York, NY: Basic Books.

Garner, Joel. (2004). *Made You Laugh: The Funniest Moments in Radio, Television, Stand-Up and Movie Comedy*. Kansas City, Missouri: Andrews McMeel.

Klein, Allen. (2010). *L.A.U.G.H.: Using Humor and Play to Help Clients Cope*. Woodbury, NY: The Guidance Group.

Leno, Jay. (2005). *How to Be the Funniest Kid in the Whole Wide World (or just in your class)*. New York, NY: Simon and Schuster.

Martin, Rod A. (2007). *The Psychology of Humor: An Integrative Approach*. Burlington, MA: Elsevier Press.

McFadyen, Ian, updated 2011 by Farrell, Karen. *Are You Trying to Be Funny? Teachers' Notes*. Melbourne International Comedy Festival Class Clowns. (History of comedy, styles of comedy, developing comedy. . .and much more) available at www.comedyfestival.com.au

McGhee, Paul. (2010). *Humor as Survival Training for a Stressed-Out World: The 7 Humor Habits Program*. Bloomington, IN: AuthorHouse.

McGhee, Paul. (2003). *Small Medium at Large: How to Develop a Powerful Verbal Sense of Humor*. (for adults). 1st Books Library.

McGhee, Paul. (2002). *Understanding and Promoting the Development of Children's Humor*. Iowa: Kendall/Hunt Publishing.

McGhee, Paul. (2002*). Stumble Bees & Pelephones: How to Develop a Powerful Verbal Sense of Humor*. Iowa: Kendall/Hunt Publishing.

Medgyes, Peter. (2002). *Laughing Matters: Humour in the Language Classroom*. Cambridge, UK: Cambridge University Press.

Morrison, Mary Kay. (2012). *Using Humor to Maximize Learning: the Links Between the Positive Emotions and Education*. Lanham, Md: Rowman & Littlefield Education.

Munsch, Robert. (2007). *Class Clown*. Markham, On: Scholastic Canada Ltd.

Nielsen, Robert. (1985). *Breeding as a Sport: 101 Student Howlers.* Available from The Book Band. www.thebookband.com

Peters, Russell. (2010). *Call Me Russell.* Toronto, On: Doubleday Canada.

Pilkey, Dav. (2012). *Captain Underpants and The Terrifying Re-turn of Tippy Tinkletrousers.* New York, NY: Scholastic.

Pollack, John. (2011). *The Pun Also Rises: How the Humble Pun Revolutionized Language, Changed History and Made Word Play More Than Some Antics.* New York, NY: Gotham Books (Penguin).

Provine, Robert R.) "Laughing, tickling and the evolution of speech and self". *Current Directions in Psychological Science.* 13,6 (December 2004): 215-18.

Purkey, William Watson. (2006). *Teaching Class Clowns (And What They Can Teach Us).* CA: Corwin Press.

Schwartz, Joel. (2006). *Noses Are Red: How to Nurture Your Child's Sense of Humor.* ADR. Book Print.

Waterson, Bill. (1995). *The Calvin and Hobbes Tenth Anniversary Book.* MI: Universal UClick.

Websites

The Canadian Association of Therapeutic Clowns—
www.therapeuticclowns.ca

The Canadian Safe School Network—www.canadiansafeschools.com

Danny Brassel—www.lazyreaders.com

Dav Pilkey and Captain Underpants book series—www.pilkey.com

Fun with Words—www.fun-with-words.com

Funny Literacy—www.humormonth.com

Giggle Poetry— www.gigglepoetry.com

Goonerisms Spalore—www.matthewgoldman.com

Helen Donnelly—www.helendonnelly.com

Holland Bloorview Kids Rehabilitation Hospital, Therapeutic Clown Program— www.bloorview.ca/programsandservices/recreationandleisure

Howard Gardner—www.howardgardner.com

The Improv Resource Centre— www.learningimprov.com/?page_id=33

Kids Help Phone—www.kidshelpphone.ca

Martin Seligman—www.authentichappiness.com

Mary Kay Morrison—www.humorquest.com

Melbourne International Comedy Festival—www.comedyfestival.com.au/2012/classclowns/www.abc.net.au

National Institute for Play—www.nifplay.com

Parenting Humor—www.parentinghumor.com

Patch Adams—www.patchadams.org

Paul McGhee—www.LaughterRemedy.com

People for Education—www.peopleforeducation.ca

Poetry for Kids—www.poetryforkids.com

Promoting Relationships and Eliminating Violence Network—www.prevnet.ca

Radical Parenting: Parenting Advice Written by Kids—www.radicalparenting.com

Sick Kids Hospital, Therapeutic Clown Program— www.sickkids.ca/therapeuticclownprogram

Steve Wilson—www.worldlaughtertour.com

Stop Bullies.com—www.stop-bullies.com

Tyler Morrison, Learn to Laugh Program—www.cottagecomedy.com

DVDs:

1. *Good Morning Miss Toliver.* PBS. (1993) 27 min.

Courses:

See Paul McGhee's online global radio humour training broadcasts
www.LaughterRemedy.com 302-897-7827

The Punch Line

"Positive education is defined as education for both traditional skills and for happiness. The high prevalence worldwide of depression among young people, the small rise in life satisfaction, and the synergy between learning and positive emotion all argue that the skills for happiness should be taught in school. There is substantial evidence from well controlled studies that skills that increase resilience, positive emotion, engagement and meaning can be taught to children." —Seligman et al

---

We all want to live as long as possible, and we also want our children to live long and healthy lives. Most people accept that moving our bodies during the day, eating more fibre, drinking more water and eating less sugar and salt are all good for overall health. While these are all important factors, recent research into longevity identifies six personality traits common to people who live longer.

- Happy
- Optimistic
- Find it easy to laugh
- Socially connected (strong relationships)
- Conscientious (persistent, detail oriented)
- Extroverted (outgoing)

—Laura Schocker, *The Huffington Post*, 2012

Note that the first four are key components of this book and feature a positive attitude towards life.

Kids have an incredible capacity for change and resilience. Positive experiences can override or undo unpleasant ones. Kids can bounce back, especially if they are made aware that life comes with pleasant and unpleasant emotions and a high degree of uncertainty. Kids need to have coping strategies and supportive parents, teachers and communities around them to manage disappointments and troublesome events.

Teaching Well-Being to Kids

We have learned more about happiness and laughter in the last ten years than in the previous hundred years. There are a growing number of cutting-edge schools and educational programs that focus on positive education. I believe that the same principles can be applied in families and relationships as well as in schools and classrooms. One example of this is The Strath Haven High School **Positive Psychology Curriculum,** a comprehensive high school curriculum that builds character strengths, relationships and meaning, in addition to raising positive emotions and reducing negative emotions. (It was developed as a pilot program with a $2.8 million grant from the U.S. Department of Education.) The two major goals of the program were to help students identify their signature character strengths and to increase their use of these strengths in their daily lives. The curriculum consisted of twenty eight-minute sessions delivered throughout the school year in grade nine.

Many of the activities in this book would be compatible with the Strath Haven Curriculum.

Here are their basic findings:

- Strengths of curiosity, love of learning and creativity were improved.
- Students' enjoyment and engagement in school increased.
- Traditional goals of classroom learning were enhanced.
- Social skills (empathy, cooperation, assertiveness and self-control) were improved.
- Bad conduct was reduced.

Another is the The Geelong Grammar School Project (Elementary) in Australia that is based on intensive teacher development—personally and professionally. Stand-alone courses are taught in several grades and the program is embedded into the entire school experience, from classes to the sports field. Each morning, grade-one students share what went well at home last night. One poignant response came from a young boy when he was asked: "Why is it important to share what went well?" He didn't hesitate: "It makes me feel good." "Anything more, Kevin?" "Oh yes, my mum asks me what went well when I get home every day, and it makes her happy when I tell her. And when Mum's happy, everybody's happy."

Pay It Forward

While you personally may not be able to start a wide-ranging community or school project like these, you can do your part to start the conversation. Share the messages of this book to friends, family, community members and workplace colleagues. Do a presentation about it. Teach the key messages in this book to children, and invite them to participate in activities that will lead them to their own discoveries about happiness, laughter and humour and put them into daily practice. Teachers can apply it in their own classrooms. Principals can encourage staff members to engage in pilot projects in different grades, especially with high-risk students. I believe all students would benefit from this additional positive psychology curriculum. Parents can apply this not only in their own homes, but can also talk about it with others in their wider family and communities. It should be the goal of both education and parenting. The benefits for children will be exciting to witness.

Life is short, and the time goes by very quickly once we are adults. Live each day like it is your last. We never know when that day will come, and we need to squeeze out every ounce of happiness and joy that we can.

My wish for you is that reading this book and doing the activities have helped you feel happier, laugh more often and tickled your own sense of humour, and that you have shared this successfully with kids and experienced a positive outcome as a parent or a teacher—or maybe even both.

Take the time to review a summary of the book's key messages:

1. The Happiness Line is a reflective reminder to gauge emotional levels.
2. Children do their best when they use their unique signature strengths.
3. Children who are positive and optimistic are more resilient.
4. Children need to express their emotions and not keep them locked up inside.
5. Happiness comes from within.
6. Laughter has physical, mental, emotional and social benefits—all aspects of wellness.
7. Children have a unique sense of humour or funprint that needs to be recognized, developed and shared with others.
8. Everyone needs permission to lighten up, play and laugh more each day.
9. Creating or performing comedy is an undervalued outlet for children's humour.
10. Comedy can be an effective coping mechanism.
11. Teasing isn't fun when it becomes hurtful and bullying is the result.
12. Structure the fun at first and then it will become more spontaneous.
13. There are many sources of support when children and families face problems.

Write or email me stories about how you used the activities in this book and what the results were for you. I intend to use my website as a place to share readers' ideas and responses as part of my blog. Does your school or community have a positive program for kids? Tell me about it. Let's join forces and work together.

As young girls, my sisters Wendy, Barb and I were regular after-school viewers of *The Roy Rogers Show* on our little television. The song *Happy Trails* that closed each episode is one of my favourite childhood memories. We would sit together right in front of the television and loudly sing along with Roy Rogers and Dale Evans. The approach to life in this song has stayed with me over my lifetime.

"Happy Trails" by Dale Evans

Happy trails to you, until we meet again.
Happy trails to you, keep smilin' until then.
Who cares about the clouds when we're together?
Just sing a song and bring the sunny weather.
Happy trails to you, 'till we meet again.

Some trails are happy ones,
Others are blue.
It's the way you ride the trail that counts,
Here's a happy one for you.

Happy trails to you, until we meet again.
Happy trails to you, keep smilin' until then.
Who cares about the clouds when we're together?
Just sing a song and bring the sunny weather.

Happy trails to you, 'till we meet again.

INDEX

D

E

F

L

M

N

O

P

Q

R